Praise for *The Art of Thriving Online*

"Amelia Knott's *The Art of Thriving Online* is a gorgeous choose-your-own-adventure for digital wellness. As someone constantly plugged in, I was captivated by Amelia's grounded, curious, nonprescriptive approach to reclaiming our digital lives.

This book is packed with realistic and fun exercises that empower you to forge your own path in the digital age. Free from a one-size-fits-all approach, through Amelia's guidance, I could feel what a healthy relationship with my phone truly means for me.

The Art of Thriving Online is not your typical self-help guide; it's a rich catalog of ways to get clear on who you are and what you want—online and offline. Amelia's insights and strategies are both refreshing and practical, providing a road map to clarity and balance in our connected world. Your free and intentional relationship with technology starts here."

Maria Bowler
coach and author of *Making Time*

"A must-read for all of us who can't decide if our phone is our most prized possession or our biggest enemy. An accessible, relatable, actionable, and tender journey of self-exploration for the chronically online, here to help us honor what the internet provides us and leave us with the tools to source what it doesn't."

Frankie Simmons
writer and host of *The Sunshine Hunter's Field Guide*

"*The Art of Thriving Online* is a road map for creative self-liberation and a warm and playful reprieve for our internet-obsessed life. Through this practical and beautiful text, Knott is a compassionate guide inviting artistic play and self-kindness. Readers learn to build a creative world that offers the respite and fulfillment they futilely seek from social media. If you struggle with social media, this is a must-read! You will feel lovingly held in Knott's vast acceptance while gently guided toward the most expressed and supported version of yourself."

Rachel Kaplan, MA, MFT
author of *Feel, Heal, and Let That Sh*t Go*

the art of thriving online

the art of *thriving* online

a workbook

creative exercises to help you
stay **grounded** + feel **joy**
in the world of **social media**

AMELIA KNOTT
RP, RCAT

sounds true
BOULDER, COLORADO

Sounds True
Boulder, CO

© 2024 Amelia Knott

Sounds True is a trademark of Sounds True Inc.
All rights reserved. No part of this book may be used or reproduced in any manner without written permission from the author and publisher.

No AI Training: Without in any way limiting the author's and publisher's exclusive rights under copyright, any use of this publication to "train" generative artificial intelligence (AI) technologies to generate text is expressly prohibited. The author reserves all rights to license uses of this work for generative AI training and development of machine learning language models.

This book is not intended as a substitute for the medical recommendations of physicians, mental health professionals, or other health-care providers. Rather, it is intended to offer information to help the reader cooperate with physicians, mental health professionals, and health-care providers in a mutual quest for optimal well-being. Art therapy combines creative processes with psychotherapy and is facilitated by credentialed mental health professionals. Although the prompts in this book have been designed by a Registered Psychotherapist and Registered Canadian Art Therapist, they are not the same as participating in art therapy. We advise readers to carefully review and understand the ideas presented and to seek the advice of a qualified professional before attempting to use them.

Published 2024

Cover design by Amelia Knott
Book design by Charli Barnes
Cover and interior illustrations © 2024 Amelia Knott

Printed in the United States of America

BK06957

ISBN: 978-1-64963-273-9

Ebook ISBN: 978-1-64963-274-6

For my dear friend Sam,

who reminds me that art cannot be contained by the language of labor,

that the here and now is to be inhabited,

and that places and things are activated by creative presence.

Acknowledging the Land

THIS IS A BOOK about mental health and the meeting place between digital and physical places. Spending time online can leave us feeling dislocated from the land we live on. Discussions of well-being cannot be separated from the social, historical, and political contexts we exist within.

I am writing from the unceded territory of the Sinixt peoples. The name of my town, Slocan, comes from the Sinixt word for spearing salmon, which were once abundant here. The Syilx, Secwépemc, and Ktunaxa peoples are also stewards of this place. As the ancestor of British and Scottish immigrants, I have unjustly benefited from my ancestors' ability to live and work on stolen land. It is the responsibility of settlers and their descendants to advocate for justice and equity for Indigenous communities who continue to be impacted by systematic displacement and oppression.

Action

If you, too, are a settler on Indigenous territory, you can participate in reconciliation by:

› learning about the Indigenous territory you live on
› exploring your own ancestral stories of migration and colonization
› reading the Truth and Reconciliation Commission of Canada's ninety-four Calls to Action[1] and the United Nations Declaration on the Rights of Indigenous Peoples[2]
› redistributing money to charities and mutual aid funds that support Indigenous people, justice, language, art, and land

Content Warning

THIS BOOK INCLUDES conversations that might be sensitive for some people. Below is a list of topics that you may wish to be aware of ahead of time. Know that you can skip sections, pause, or seek support if any of these discussions feels activating for you.

Chapter 3 mentions:

› racism and police brutality
› transphobia and harassment of LGBTQIA2S+ advocates
› exploitation of children in family vlogging
› violence in Gaza and censorship of Palestinian activists
› violence toward Indigenous women and girls and censorship of Indigenous activists

Chapter 4 mentions:

› body shame and fatphobia
› disability and physical differences
› exercises inviting somatic awareness

Chapter 5 mentions:

› harassment of women working in the tech industry
› Islamophobia and the Rohingya Muslim genocide in Myanmar
› gun violence and the Pizzagate conspiracy
› the 2023 Dublin anti-immigration riots
› descriptions of a pro-life protest
› the 2016 American presidential election

Chapter 6 mentions:

› exercises inviting somatic awareness
› the body's responses to trauma
› eco-grief and climate anxiety

Exploring our mental health and creating art can bring up uncomfortable feelings. You don't need to face those feelings alone. It may be valuable to work with a mental health professional while you explore your relationship with social media. You can find a directory of professional art therapists who work online and in person in the US and Canada through the Canadian Art Therapy Association (canadianarttherapy.org) and American Art Therapy Association (arttherapy.org). If you are concerned for your safety or are in need of immediate support, you can find help by phone or text through a crisis line.[1]

Sponsored by the International Association for Suicide Prevention, Find a Helpline is a free online tool that easily connects people to helplines in more than fifty countries.

Find a Helpline: iasp.info/crisis-centres-helplines

Before You Begin

DO YOU EVER freeze at the beginning of a new journal or sketchbook, worried that the first page needs to be something beautiful or profound? Before we even begin, let's do away with that pressure. Destroy this page as an opening ceremony for a process that is allowed to be messy, imperfect, uncertain, and authentic.

SCRIBBLE!

FOLD OR CRUMPLE THIS PAGE!

SPILL YOUR COFFEE HERE!

RIP IT INTO TINY PIECES!

Contents

Introduction: A New Way toward Digital Wellness   1

CHAPTER 1:   Attention   13

CHAPTER 2:   Productivity + Urgency   35

CHAPTER 3:   Privacy + Performance   77

CHAPTER 4:   Comparison + Worthiness   121

CHAPTER 5:   Fear + Anger + Disinformation   161

CHAPTER 6:   Place + Body + Belonging   201

CHAPTER 7:   Stitching It All Together   249

Conclusion   265

Acknowledgments   267

Notes   269

Book Club Guide   275

About the Author   279

INTRODUCTION

A New Way toward Digital Wellness

I wish I could just quit social media.

This is a sentence I hear often in my practice as an art therapist. It makes sense to me that so many of us grapple with our relationships with our phones—social media is entwined with countless aspects of our daily lives—but it is not designed with our psychological well-being in mind. Digital platforms, including social media, news channels, search engines, and e-commerce apps, are designed to capitalize on our vulnerability.

Social media changes how we focus and where we direct our attention. It asks us to be reachable at all times, blurring the lines between work and home. It asks us to perform a lifestyle instead of inhabiting our lives. Social media suspends us in a perpetual state of urgency that doesn't dissolve when our phones are turned off—if they ever get turned off. It pressures us to keep up with every news story, every conflict, every controversy, every status update, every notification. It fortifies divisions and distorts truth. The sheer volume of information we're inundated with every day is enough to make anyone feel unwell.

Being on social media can leave us feeling overwhelmed, anxious, lonely, numb, enraged, and unworthy. So, why do we stay online?

When my clients explain what stops them from quitting social media once and for all, I hear them share all kinds of valid, thoughtful reasons, such as . . .

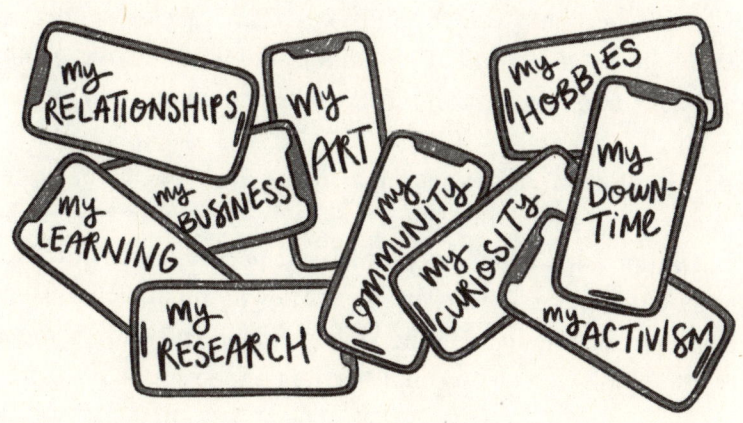

These are not small needs. Social media has the power to make us feel unwell, *and* it is also a very real source of connection, conversation, and community.

Our digital lives are meaningful, but they are also complicated, posing daily threats to our sense of self and belonging. Holding the paradox of the danger and the usefulness of social media, how do we care for our mental health? How do we stay connected to each other while feeling a sense of awareness, choice, and even joy? How might we advocate for a digital future driven by equity and care? What would it mean to stay online *and* create a conscious relationship with social media?

The answer begins with the word *create*. Through creativity, we can rethink and re-create the ways we live in the online social realm. Creativity is the quality that helps us imagine different futures, and with creativity, reflection, and awareness, we can find innovative ways to preserve the goodness and usefulness of our time online—not just for ourselves, but for the collective.

Wellness Is a Wounded Word

Today, when I search #wellness on social media, the results are dominated by green smoothies; spas; supplements; and thin, white bodies. The ways we understand wellness have been shaped by the ways we communicate. Since social media centers images and videos, currently, we conceptualize wellness through the lens of what can be shown rather than what can be felt. Wellness has become a ubiquitous buzzword that gestures vaguely toward a narrow definition of health and status.

It's challenging to untangle what wellness actually feels like when we encounter incessant digital messaging about who we should be, what we should look like, and how we should live. This messaging can leave us wondering, *What is wrong with me? If I am doing all the things—taking the bath, drinking the tea, doing the journaling, reposting the affirmations, embarking on the digital detox—shouldn't I feel better?*

This approach doesn't look upstream to the sources of our suffering. It doesn't factor in aspects of our lives that can't simply be overridden with routines and willpower. These factors might be personal, like chronic illness, neurodivergence, or traumatic experiences. They might also be systemic, like racism, capitalism, colonialism, homophobia, or ableism. Addressing and confronting the complex web of personal barriers and systems of oppression *is* the work of wellness. This inner work and systemic work are harder to document and display online.

The digital wellness industry would also have us believe that thriving is a solitary journey. Our culture loves to tell the story of an individual who persisted alone against adversity. Online, healing becomes a performance of personal ascension and achievement. The problem with this type of self-care and self-help rhetoric is that it begins and ends with the self. It doesn't connect us to others who share in our experience. It doesn't motivate or mobilize us toward changing the status quo.

Here are the ways I understand wellness and the values behind this workbook:

› Wellness is **relational**. It is built when we tend to our relationships with others by both seeking and offering support.
› Wellness is about **liberation** for all, not just a privileged few. Mental health is a political conversation.
› Wellness is supported by **creativity**. Making things is a way of experiencing our agency, our truth, and our humanity.

Now you get to decide what wellness feels like for you. This workbook is about creating a definition that includes the unique contexts of your life.

It is for you. It is for all of us.

A New Narrative about Wellness on Social Media

In 2011, two-thirds of Syria's internet access was shut down without notice, in response to mounting unrest at the beginning of a civil war.[1] Following censorship efforts, the United Nations declared access to the internet a basic human right. Their report emphasized how internet access "contributes to the discovery of the truth and progress of society as a whole."[2] Some countries have built this human right into legislation. In 2009, Finland mandated that citizens are entitled to internet connection with a speed of at least one megabit per second.

Though this workbook focuses on social media, virtually every aspect of our lives is touched by the internet. Being online isn't just about our social lives; it's crucial to how we interface with the world around us.

The challenge is that these tools enabling freedom of opinion and expression are not built upon those same virtues. Algorithms create unseen architectures that influence how we communicate, how we shop, how we receive news, how we vote, and how we perceive what is true. To speak technically, an algorithm is a set of encoded rules enabling technology to automate decisions about what is shared. Algorithms use artificial intelligence to perform tasks that, in the past, would have required human intelligence, like moderating content. They also employ machine learning to sort and analyze data about your online behavior and the behavior of your contacts. They also make predictions about the types of content you are most likely to engage with. Algorithms are programmed to analyze personal data to refine their strategies.

Your newsfeed is a bespoke domain—customized to captivate, provoke, nudge, and continually monitor your actions to craft an increasingly irresistible user experience.

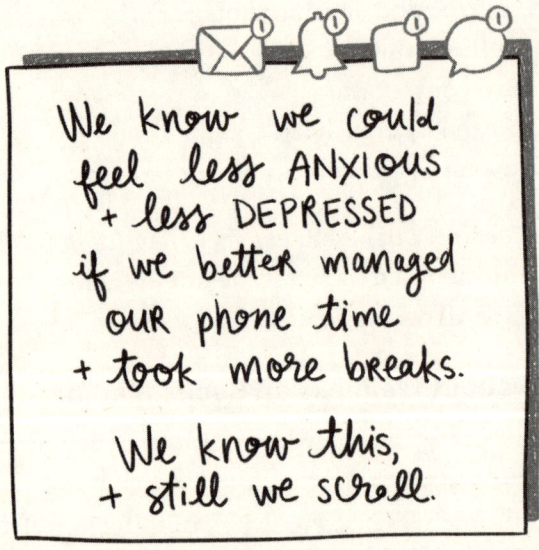

We know we could feel less ANXIOUS + less DEPRESSED if we better managed our phone time + took more breaks.

We know this, + still we scroll.

Thriving online isn't just about trying to spend less time scrolling. It is about maintaining your mental health when you choose to sign on by becoming aware of the invisible influences shaping your thoughts and feelings.

Most self-help books agree that leaving or drastically limiting social media is the clearest road to well-being. They offer strategies for reducing screen time and make compelling arguments for deleting your profiles altogether.

I agreed with these strategies until the pandemic. Before 2020, I had drawn a line between my "real life" and the time I spent online. I once did this literally by taping a red boundary on the floor of my studio apartment between my bedroom and my kitchen, promising myself that I wouldn't stare at a screen in the part of my home that was meant for resting. (This worked for less than a week.)

During the first cycles of pandemic isolation, I noticed that social media felt different than it had before. With my family far away, I relied on technology to remain tethered in my relationships. Zoom rooms became my classrooms, dance floors, community halls, and art studios. Digital communities became my safest sources of belonging. I no longer had the option to practice art therapy in person, and social media opened possibilities for working online. Of course, this expanded usefulness wasn't first discovered as we sheltered in place in the early months of 2020. The accessibility and connective potential of the internet has long been utilized by people for whom the world is less than welcoming. For decades, those experiencing isolation due to factors like chronic illness, prejudice, or displacement have stewarded vibrant online communities. But for many people, the pandemic changed the role social media plays in our lives; it became a vital space that actually supported our wellness.

The advice to simply quit or detox from social media underestimates the role these tools now play in many of our lives. The ability to even consider leaving takes a certain amount of social and financial leverage. By this, I mean it is easier to choose a path of limiting social media use if you have certain privileges.

Can you get your needs for connection and care met through your in-person relationships alone? Do you live in a place where building a like-minded, in-person community is easy? Does face-to-face interaction feel safe and comfortable to you? Could you financially support yourself without the networking and advertising tools built into social media? Do you have an offline platform large enough to sustain the work you do? Does your work require keeping up with the news cycle, current research, or pop culture? Are digital spaces your most accessible sources of fun and entertainment?

Our lives are entwined with social media for so many reasons. We may choose to use social media because it is the safest, easiest, or most sustainable way to meet our basic needs—and a sense of belonging *is* a basic need. Having all our social and financial needs met offline is a type of privilege not everyone has access to. Many of us are not positioned to thrive without the tools social media offers us.

I am not saying social media can—or should—replace our in-person relationships. The conversation has become more nuanced than the binary belief that social media is plainly bad for us. "Just quit" is no longer helpful advice when our lives are so entrenched with digital tools. We are ready for a new narrative—one that tells the truth about why we use social media, how it impacts us, and who benefits from our screen time. We need a narrative that honors the value we find both online and offline.

My Positionality

I'm writing this workbook from the perspective of a person with many privileged intersections of identity. My life and worldview have been shaped by the unearned advantages of being a white, cis settler. My hope is that by including the voices of writers, therapists, artists, and thinkers with different lived experiences from my own, this workbook will speak widely to those exploring what it means to care for their mental health online.

Most important, I do not have all the answers. Though my writing is informed by my work and training as a psychotherapist and art therapist, I don't believe there is a single intervention or perspective to address this problem. In my fifteen years of using social media, I've tried dozens of strategies for controlling my screen time. These days, I am less interested in discovering the mythical *one thing* that works. Claiming to have definitive answers is a good way to sell hope (and books), but similar to diets and pyramid schemes, those who don't find "success" will wonder if something is deeply wrong with them. Instead of pursuing certainty, I feel devoted to being with the question of why screens are so captivating, how they impact my sense of wellness in the world, and how to build a relationship with social media that I don't need to escape.

Instead of telling you exactly what to do or how I permanently fixed my relationship with social media (I haven't! My screen time was up 23 percent last week!), this is a space for you to find your own answers and author your own definition of wellness—online and offline. Your authentic expressions and reflections will be far more valuable than any prescriptive strategy I could assume would work for you. This workbook is designed to help you guide yourself.

This Isn't the End-All Solution

This workbook will *not* help you:

> fix yourself—you're not broken!
> promise a "perfect" or one-size-fits-all digital detox
> tell you the right answers

This Is a Starting Point for a New Relationship

This workbook will help you:

> carve out space in your life to reflect on your relationship with social media
> learn to use art materials to explore and express emotions
> think critically about your digital habits
> learn about the ways technology impacts your mental health and relationships
> explore the political and economic motivations shaping social media
> unpack systemic barriers to personal and collective wellness
> author an authentic definition of well-being online

How to Use This Workbook

This workbook is organized into chapters that explore:

1. Attention
2. Productivity + Urgency
3. Privacy + Performance
4. Comparison + Worthiness
5. Fear + Anger + Disinformation
6. Place + Body + Belonging

At the end of this workbook, you will write your own Gentle Manifesto. This is not another to-do list or a shiny, new self-care regimen, but rather a chance to create a personal philosophy of time well spent. This workbook will help you gather your insights from each chapter and craft a personal statement of what online wellness feels like for you.

In Each Chapter, You Will Find

STORIES + RESEARCH:

We'll explore how art, psychology, history, and digital culture relate to mental health. We'll also hear from the artists, writers, and researchers who are shaping these conversations.

CREATIVE INVITATIONS:

This workbook will invite you to scribble, cut, rearrange, draw, doodle, fill in the blanks, and much more. I use the word *invitation* for creative prompts because it offers choice. There are no requirements in the book except to make it work for you! If you would like to try creating in a way that is different from my instructions, that's amazing! Follow your intuition and express yourself in any way that feels right for you.

REFLECTION QUESTIONS:

Journaling questions will help you dive deeper into understanding your relationship with social media and the meaning behind your creative expressions. Use the space in this workbook to write and reflect. There are no wrong answers here!

ART THERAPIST TIPS:

I'll pop in once in a while to share a fact or insight from the perspective of art psychotherapy.

HACKS THAT HELP:

I've crowdsourced a few tips and tricks. These are practical strategies that some people find helpful for managing their relationships with technology.

HARVEST EXERCISES:

There is a lot to explore and absorb in this workbook. With that in mind, here are some of the key exercise elements that will repeat as chapter-ending creative invitations. In the final chapter of the workbook, you'll use these harvest exercises to inform your Gentle Manifesto.

› **Questions:** To help you gather more meaning from your art and writing, the harvest sections open with key questions. It's not about what you should take away, but what you might continue to ponder in order to deepen your reflections.
› **Playlist:** Music is a powerful way to connect with your emotions. You'll make a playlist based on the themes that arise in each chapter.
› **Find the Gift:** Allow your effort to reward you! You'll distill your reflections by imagining the gift, wisdom, or advice you'd like to carry forward with you. These gifts will come together in the Gentle Manifesto when you throw yourself a party.
› **Quilt Square:** You'll color in a quilt square to represent your takeaways in each chapter. By the time you reach the end of this workbook, you will have created six squares to cut and paste into a quilt as a way of "sewing together" your experience.

Other Things to Consider

YOU GET TO CHOOSE YOUR SPEED AND RHYTHM:

As a person with attention deficit hyperactivity disorder (ADHD), I often start projects with a lot of energy and then work on them sporadically over a long period of time. (My craft-supply inventory can attest to this!) Perhaps it would feel right to carve out time on Saturday mornings to work through each chapter. Perhaps you keep this workbook in your backpack to use on your morning commute. Perhaps you reach for this workbook once every few months and skip some invitations entirely. What would it feel like to give yourself permission to work through these pages at whatever pace and rhythm feels natural? What would it feel like to release the pressure to "do it right"? You have my enthusiastic, neurodivergent permission to half-ass it.

YOU GET TO CHOOSE HOW YOU CREATE:

If you find that certain topics, activities, or ways of expressing aren't comfortable or possible for you right now, then adapt this workbook to work for you. If typing is more accessible than handwriting, use a computer or phone for journaling activities. If speaking is more accessible than writing, explore prompts in a conversation with a trusted friend or a voice memo to yourself. It's always an option to pause or skip invitations.

YOU GET TO CHOOSE WHAT YOU CREATE WITH:

You can complete the invitations in this book with simple art materials like felt pens, pencils, or crayons. But if you feel called to use a different material, have at it! Grab some glitter! Cut up a magazine and glue in pictures! Build up thick layers of paint! All expressions are welcome.

YOU GET TO CHOOSE WHO YOU SHARE YOUR CREATIONS WITH:

It might feel good to share your experience of working through this workbook with others. It might also feel good to keep it completely to yourself. You may change your mind from page to page! Art can be personal and vulnerable. If you're a person who likes to share your self-discovery journeys on social media, pay attention to how you may censor yourself when you anticipate posting your process. Know that you can choose who gets to see and hear your expressions.

Gentle Accountability

I have a hard time sustaining momentum alone. If you'd like to create accountability around this process, try working through this workbook in a group. This is a great way to take your explorations off the page and into your life and community. At the back of this book, you will find a book-club guide with suggestions for fun ways to organize meetings and explore these topics with other people.

Soft Work

Each chapter of this workbook ends with a quilt square.

I used to think about the internet in metaphors like webs and nets—things that organize, tangle, and offer an almost-invisible utility. But these days, when I think about social media's evolving role in my life and the culture at large, I think about making a quilt.

Quilting involves choosing shapes and textures, finding ways to make them fit, and joining them together. Quilting takes time and is often done in community; it's soft work that culminates in an object of comfort, warmth, and legacy.

If the internet makes up the fabric of our lives, then we might think of ourselves as quilters. What swatches of fabric do we want to choose? What story does the pattern tell? What actually *feels* good to hold against our bodies? What do we want to drape around the shoulders of the ones we love? What techniques will we choose to ensure the quilt can be passed down to future generations?

How can we stitch together the facets of our digital lives to create something that supports us in feeling well?

Here's the thing about quilts: I don't actually know how to make one. What I do know is that you can pull a needle and thread through squares of fabric without a plan for exactly how the material will take shape. You can start with skills you already possess and discover as you go. I also know that the repetitive motion of making one stitch and then another transports me back into the here and now.

Whether you are creating a quilt without instructions or grappling with the unknowns of a future shaped by algorithms and artificial intelligence, you can simply begin by intending toward a hope for comfort and true connection. We can allow the soft work of staying with our questions to grow into something we couldn't have envisioned at the start.

So, let's begin.

CHAPTER 1

ATTENTION

It's Not You. It's Media.

Have you ever picked up your phone to check the time and realized that twenty minutes passed before you knew it? You read an article on the sleeping habits of seahorses, added and then removed a bullet journal from your Amazon cart, watched a sock-mending tutorial on TikTok, and you *still* don't know what time it is.

Sometimes I berate myself when I realize that my attention has once again been colonized by a screen. I think to myself, grumpy and exasperated, *Why can't I just put down my phone!?* My frustration isn't purely about the hours I can't reclaim. The voice in my head is burdened with beliefs about what my screen time must mean about who I am as a person. These beliefs sound like, *If I were smarter, stronger, and more disciplined, I wouldn't be so susceptible to this distraction. Other people don't struggle with their phones like this. I am weak. I am unintelligent. I am lazy. There is something wrong with me.*

It makes sense that my internal dialogue is so critical. Social media platforms are designed to fragment our attention. When we use these apps, we are bombarded with stimuli from all directions. This barrage of information is, of course, intentional.

For example, if I open an app to search for a recipe, I may be greeted with a video that plays automatically. This video has been selected for me based on the app's observations of what I'm most likely to engage with. I can't help but read the text overlaying the quick jump cuts between video clips. The creator of that content likely knows they have just a few moments to persuade me to keep watching, so they begin with a hook: *5 reasons why . . . , Here's a life-hack for . . . , Try this one simple trick . . .* After another moment, a bar of red notifications appears to let me know six people have left comments on something I posted, I've been mentioned in a video, and someone is waiting for me to reply to a message. These cyber-siren songs beckon me toward the rocky shores of distraction.

My attention didn't stand a chance. In a matter of seconds, my original mission of finding a recipe is swept away in a torrent of content, and my mind feels a little like a scrambled egg. Holding our attention in one place while on social media is like trying to thread a needle on a roller coaster. We enter a space that is not designed to foster concentration. In fact, it's designed to do the opposite. Knowing this, it's understandable that I feel frustrated with myself when I finally emerge from the fog of stimuli—still unsure how long it takes to cook couscous.

We're going to begin by exploring our relationship with attention. Don't worry—this is not a conversation about simply strengthening our willpower. Practicing digital wellness involves cultivating an awareness of *how* our attention is deliberately manipulated. It also means offering ourselves grace when social media does exactly what it is designed to do: fracture our focus and keep us scrolling.

Attention Audit

We can bring awareness to social media's impact on our focus by doing an *attention audit*. This is a way of taking stock of where we're spending our energy, both online and offline. Auditing our own patterns of attention gives us a better picture of how we spend our lives. Once we're aware of the landscapes we're living in, we can decide whether we want to inhabit the space, change it, or migrate elsewhere.

When I guided participants of a workshop through these activities, some people were shocked by how saturated their feeds were with upsetting news stories. Other people noticed how boring they actually found updates about strangers' lunches and vacations. The point of an attention audit isn't to judge ourselves or come to conclusions about whether our digital habits are "good" or "bad"; it's about collecting data with curiosity so we're better able to understand our relationships with social media.

Try a mini attention audit to get started:

Reflect:

Without looking, how would you describe the types of social media accounts and content you surround yourself with?

_____

_____

_____

_____

Now open your most-used social media app and take a look at the first five pieces of content. Notice both the user-generated content and the ads.

On _____ *(fill in the site or app)*, I saw:

1. _____
2. _____
3. _____
4. _____
5. _____

What did this app or site actually show you? What feelings do you notice after even a quick look at your feed?

_____

_____

_____

_____

ATTENTION 15

Doodle Graph

If your attention throughout the day were a line, what would it look like? Draw a line that changes by the hour to show the ups and downs of your attention. Add details that help explain the things that impact your focus.

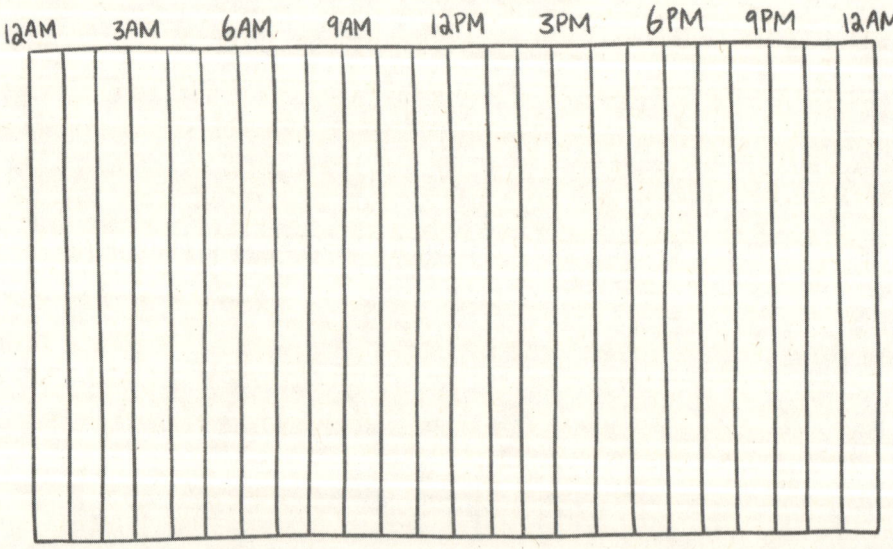

Distraction Hall of Fame

In a culture that prizes productivity, it's tempting to demonize distraction. However, finding respite from the intensity of life is also crucial to our well-being. Distractions can get in the way, *and* they can also be a joyful reprieve.

Draw your award-winning distractions inside these ribbons:

Now that you've had a preview of the kinds of content you regularly engage with, let's dive deeper into the ways social media holds our attention.

The Attention Economy

Putting down our phones can feel hard, not simply because we lack willpower or focus but because online spaces are engineered to hold our attention for as long as possible. In her book *How to Do Nothing*, Jenny Odell describes the perils of the attention economy by explaining that "platforms such as Facebook and Instagram act like dams that capitalize on our natural interest in others and an ageless need for community, hijacking and frustrating our most innate desires, and profiting from them."[1] In other words, the attention economy refers to the industries and technologies that profit from and commodify users' attention. The longer we spend reading an article or scrolling through an app, the more opportunities there are for data gatherers to analyze our behavior and advertise to us, redirect us, and keep us mesmerized.

This is why we get to use social media for free. It's not that we are *using* a product when we're online; it's that our attention *is* the product being sold to larger companies. As you can imagine, digital platforms have financial incentives to keep people on their sites for as long as possible.

This is where the dark side of psychology comes in.

In a 2017 talk, Sean Parker, the first president of Facebook, described the rationale of attention-holding design saying, "The thought process that went into building the applications—Facebook being the first of them—was all about: 'How do we consume as much of your time and conscious attention as possible?' And that means that we need to sort of give you a little dopamine hit every once in a while because someone liked or commented on a photo or a post or whatever."[2]

Dopamine is a neurotransmitter responsible for the brain's ability to pursue rewards. When we engage in pleasurable experiences like eating, sex, exercise, and positive social connection, the brain releases dopamine. Similarly, activities and substances that provoke thrills, euphoria, or adrenaline are motivated by these same brain functions. Over time, as we learn to associate pleasure with certain behaviors, even the anticipation of them will trigger a dopamine response. This is how habits are reinforced by repetition and why cravings can feel so overwhelming. This is also why it can feel so uncomfortable not to receive a reward we have come to expect. Our brains experience a negative prediction error with the spike in dopamine that comes from anticipating a reward, followed by a decrease in dopamine when we don't receive it.

Knowing this, the engineers of persuasive technologies also implement variable rewards into the designs of their apps. At casinos, slot machines use the same psychology to keep gamblers playing as long as possible. Slot machines exploit the fact that we are likely to repeat a high-dopamine behavior if we aren't certain if or when we will win. On social media, variable rewards arrive in the form of notifications, released in bursts to keep you checking back. Refreshing your feed is akin to gambling with your dopamine.

It's challenging to put our phones down because we are hardwired to seek out connection and satisfaction. Human beings are social creatures, not just because connection feels good, but because our lives depend on it. Throughout history, our survival has been linked to an ability to maintain community and monitor the risk of exclusion. As a result, our bodies register feelings of belonging and approval from others as safety. It makes sense that a device offering frequent and unpredictable doses of a type of belonging would captivate our attention in such a powerful way.

Research also shows that our ability to multitask (or switch efficiently between tasks) is limited. It takes valuable energy to refocus on an intended task once our attention has drifted elsewhere.

The takeaway is that your willpower is not the real villain in your battle with your phone. Behind every screen there are teams of thousands of software engineers and behavioral psychologists—not to mention billions of dollars invested in maximizing your screen time.

We will continue to explore the ways social media platforms impact our wellness throughout this workbook. For now, let's begin by paying attention to the places our attention goes.

Seek and Find: A Sensory Treasure Hunt

The physical objects you choose to surround yourself with are clues that will help you create a personal definition of what actually feels good. Although this workbook is about your digital environment, paying attention to your physical environment will also offer some valuable hints about what makes a space feel safe and comfortable for you.

We make conscious and unconscious choices every day about our surroundings. The types of fabric we wear, the size of spoon we choose (small spoon always—if you know, you know), and the things we keep in the fridge are not accidental. They all reflect our sensory preferences. In this sensory scavenger hunt, move through your home and notice the smells, colors, textures, and moods you feel best around. Getting granular about the sensations your body enjoys is not a frivolous task. Sensory pleasure and comfort are important facets of well-being.

Take this workbook with you as you walk through your home. Invite the voice of David Attenborough—the British broadcaster, author, and natural historian—to narrate in your head as you explore. Find your favorite things to see, hear, touch, smell, and taste. For every item you choose, pick two more words to describe a feeling or association you have with that object.

Example:

SENSE	OBJECTS	DESCRIPTIONS
smell	candle	earthy, warm
taste	lemon seltzer	effervescent, bright
touch	mom's sweater	cozy, nostalgic
see	house plants	green, alive
hear	dance playlist	groovy, buoyant

Go on a sensory scavenger hunt:

SENSE	OBJECTS	DESCRIPTION
smell	• • •	
taste	• • •	
touch	• • •	
see	• • •	
hear	• • •	

art therapist tip:

Go with Your Felt Sense

It's normal to feel stumped when you're trying to describe your gut response to an image or feeling. If you find yourself getting hung up on choosing the perfect word to explain an experience, know that you can go with your *felt sense*. This means writing down the very first thing that comes to mind, even if you can't explain why it feels correct. Maybe the smell of your office reminds you of your second-grade teacher. Maybe the feeling of the rug under your feet brings the word *spunchy* to mind. That's a word I just invented, and I have no idea what it means, but it registers in my body as correct.

Does it matter that you don't know exactly why you have a certain association? Not at all! Language is inherently limiting. Play with words and phrases that point toward an abstract feeling. Oftentimes the first thing that pops into your head is gesturing toward a personal truth. What matters is that you're listening to your inner sense of what just *feels* true.

Search and Discover: Digital Scavenger Hunt

Now we're going to gather some data from your digital environment. Let's pay attention to your reactions to the types of content you see regularly online.

Step 1

Open the social media platform you use most regularly. This will work best if you use a platform that automatically suggests content or accounts based on your viewing history (which is most of them!).

Step 2

Set a timer and spend fifteen minutes scrolling. Each time you come across a new image, video, status, headline, or ad, write down the very first two words that come to mind. These words could describe the content or your reaction to it. Your reaction might be a word that describes what you see, an emotion you feel, or a random association. There are no wrong answers!

Example:

CONTENT:	DESCRIPTION WORDS:
video of a dog eating ice cream	wholesome, laughter

Scroll, notice, and describe:

CONTENT:	DESCRIPTION WORDS:

ATTENTION 23

Step 3

Are there any other words that describe your experience of scrolling that you would like to add to your list?

_____
_____
_____

What did you notice about the types of content you just saw?

_____
_____
_____

What emotions, thoughts, or sensations do you notice in your body right now? Are they different from fifteen minutes ago?

_____
_____
_____
_____

If the sensations in your body had a voice, what might they ask you for right now? A stretch? A glass of water? Fifteen more minutes of scrolling?

_____
_____
_____
_____

art therapist tip:

The Noticing Break

"What am I noticing right now?" is a magic question. It centers you in the here and now. This question can help you focus on your body, your emotions, and the environment around you. Practicing being present like this—especially when we're online—can help us step aside from any stories we are telling ourselves and just be.

Analyze the Data

Take this data back to the lab for analysis. It's time to get curious about the information you gathered in your sensory and digital scavenger hunts.

SENSORY SCAVENGER HUNT DESCRIPTION WORDS	DIGITAL SCAVENGER HUNT DESCRIPTION WORDS

› In the left box, write down the description words from your sensory treasure hunt.
› In the right box, write the description words from your digital treasure hunt.
› Circle or underline your favorite words from both categories.

Reflect:

What do you notice about these two sets of words? How are these words similar? How are they different?

_____

_____

_____

_____

Now that you have collected some sets of data, let's get curious about how you feel about these words.

Do you notice any beliefs or judgments about these words? Do they feel true? Do you wish they were different? Simply notice what thoughts and feelings arise.

_____

_____

_____

_____

_____

_____

_____

Tend to Your Garden

Imagine that your favorite words from both your sensory and digital scavenger hunts are seeds planted in a garden. Write the words inside the seeds below and envision what they might need to grow. Draw anything that will help them thrive in the space surrounding them.

If a seed needs boundaries or protection, you might draw something like a fence or a guard dog. If a seed craves encouragement or care, you might draw something that offers nourishment, like the sun or a watering can. Allow this drawing to become a full and flourishing garden.

ATTENTION

HACKS THAT HELP

- I switched to a flip phone that doesn't have internet access.

- I outsourced my willpower by installing an app that blocks me from using social media between 9:00 p.m. and 9:00 a.m.

- I use an app that prompts me to take a deep breath and wait ten seconds before I can open TikTok. In that moment, I can decide if I really want to be online instead of scrolling unconsciously.

- I bought an alarm clock so I don't accidentally end up checking social media when I go to turn off my phone alarm.

- I write my weekly screen time on a sticky note so I have a reminder of the hours I actually spend online.

- I set my phone to black-and-white display. It's a lot less captivating without color!

- I bought a kitchen safe with a timer and lock my phone inside. When I need to focus, I set the lockbox for an hour or two.

- I got a landline. I shared my phone number with people who might need to contact me during hours that my cell phone is in time-out.

HARVEST

Use these activities to help you distill your reflections about how social media shapes your attention. It might be useful to look back at your art and writing as you harvest meaning from this chapter.

Playlist: Songs for Attention

Take a moment to browse through music you enjoy, and pick:

› A song for when you're in the mood for a fun distraction

_____

_____

› A song to play in the background when you want to focus

_____

_____

› A song that reminds you to have compassion for yourself

_____

_____

Find the Gift

Imagine your attention audit has a gift for you. It might be an affirmation, a revelation, or a superpower to take with you into your future digital life. Draw it here.

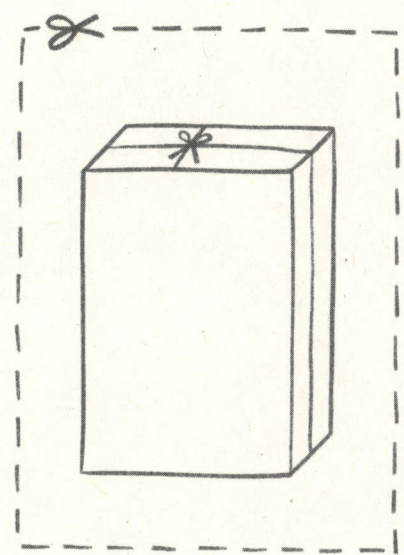

Quilt Square

Fill in the center square of this quilt block with a color or pattern to represent the things in life you want to pay attention to. In the outside spaces, choose colors or patterns to symbolize the things that distract you from what's meaningful.

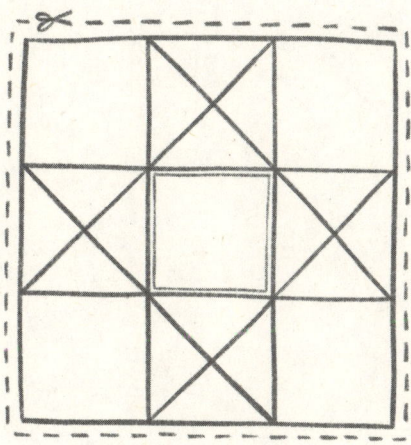

SNIP! SNIP!

CHAPTER 2

PRODUCTIVITY + URGENCY

"It's Wednesday, Come Get Ready with Me."

I imagine an anthropology student in the year 2100 sharing a presentation with her peers on feminist labor movements of the previous century. The student presents a cultural relic of the mid-2020s—the five-to-nine *Get Ready with Me Vlog*. Before playing a sample video, she explains to her peers, "It was common for social media users, especially women, to make short documentary-style videos about their early-morning routines."

The student begins by noting the video's pace—how quickly the creator lists the tasks of her morning with rehearsed nonchalance. She points out the incongruence between the composure of the narration and the frantic sequence of tasks, describing the "performance of equanimity projected onto the backdrop of urgent labor and consumption." The video shows tropes of the era: the seventeen-step skin-care artillery, the standing desk placed over a treadmill, the oat milk foam swirling into iced coffee with a glass straw. The students watching the presentation giggle at the creator's now-retro yoga pants and the dated ASMR-style audio.

The anthropology student unpacks the common narratives that were expressed in these videos. Women often described their exhaustion, their resistance, and their motivation for rising early. They described treasuring those quiet hours: a deliberate protection of moments alone to care for their minds and bodies before the demands for their domestic, emotional, and intellectual labor began for the day. The student explains that these videos depict that labor too. Women documented their predawn cooking and cleaning, their goal-setting, their diets, their journaling, and even their meditation. This particular style of vlog revealed the unseen effort of working women, while ironically concealing the labor spent performing, documenting, and editing depictions of their lives. The student pauses by noting that the video ends with the *beginning* of the creator's day.

I like to imagine that the class then discusses how much has changed in the years since the video was made, the same way we might discuss how attitudes about women's roles in the home have shifted since the 1950s. In my imagination, these students exist in a future where productivity isn't code for worthiness.

At the time I am writing this workbook, we are four years into a global pandemic. The culture of work has shifted dramatically—not just for people who identify as women, but for everyone. By June of 2020, 42 percent of American workers had begun performing their jobs from home, accounting for more than 60 percent of the nation's economic activity.[1] For those privileged enough to work from home, the remaining boundary between work and life collapsed. In April of the following year, a record-breaking number of Americans joined "The Great Resignation" by quitting their jobs.[2] As workers faced the threat of illness, economic precarity, and a rapidly evolving culture of employment, it's no surprise that, for the past four years, the self-help book charts have been dominated by titles promising to help readers increase their productivity. In "unprecedented" times, it makes sense that we would be captivated by conversations that relate to our sense of safety in the world. We cannot control how rapidly a virus mutates and spreads, but maybe we can multitask and hack ourselves into the illusion of security. The ongoing popularity of pyramid schemes promising a lucrative side hustle is a symptom of our deeply human desire to find a pathway out of precarity. Why unionize or demand a universal basic income when you, too, could have your first six-figure month coaching coaches to coach coaches?

Social media throws gasoline on our societal values and our fears. It's funny to think of an influencer's five-to-nine routine video as a historical artifact, but the prevalence of this type of narrative points to a theme in the collective consciousness: we need to get more done, we need to make more money, we need to demonstrate our value in the workforce, we need to find a foothold of security as we face social and economic uncertainty. Right on cue, social media holds a magnifying glass over our anxiety, and our feeds deliver an endless stream of examples of people embracing the "grindset" to optimize their time, attention, and willpower. In this chapter, we'll explore what it could mean to divest from hyper-productivity and allow ourselves to truly rest.

Reflect:

What role does productivity play in your life? What are your associations with this word? Fill in this mind map to brainstorm your association with this word.

How does social media impact the way you feel about your productivity? Reflect on the types of content that inspire you versus the types that leave you feeling "less than." It's okay if these lists aren't static! The same post might land differently day to day, depending on your mood.

The type of content that usually makes me feel motivated is . . .

_____

_____

_____

_____

_____

_____

_____

The type of content that usually makes me feel inadequate is . . .

_____

_____

_____

_____

_____

_____

_____

Make Your Meme

The caption on my all-time favorite meme reads: "Stop glamorizing 'the grind' and start glamorizing whatever this is." The picture that follows is an illustration of Mr. Frog and Mr. Toad riding a tandem bicycle (from the *Frog and Toad* series of children's books written and illustrated by Arnold Lobel).³ I've seen other equally wholesome versions of this meme with pictures of old men playing chess in a hot spring, a mouse reading in a rocking chair, and LARPers (live-action-role-players) holding foam swords with wide grins. What activity, feeling, or experience would *you* like to glamorize?

Create a collage meme of what you would like to glamorize instead of productivity. Gather old photos, pictures from magazines, junk mail, or old art, and glue them in the space below to create a meme of a scene worth celebrating.

PRODUCTIVITY + URGENCY

Social Media + the Rise of Hustle Culture

The urgency of Hustle Culture is not limited to what we believe we should accomplish; it's also the information we should digest and the content we should produce. *The news cycle is updated by the second. Your phone pings with an email from your boss at 10:30 p.m. Your followers want to know if part 2 of your video series is posted yet. Your language app shames you for failing to complete a lesson today. The* New York Times *weighs in on the election.* When life moves at the speed of the algorithm, it's hard to pause long enough to wonder if *productivity* is really the metric we want to measure our lives against.

Tricia Hersey, the founder of The Nap Ministry, offers a revolutionary reframe. Founded in 2016, The Nap Ministry is a social justice organization that uses art to disrupt the culture of overwork perpetuated by capitalism and white supremacy. Through performance, installation, and community care, The Nap Ministry invites deeper conversations about rest as a human right, especially for folks most impacted by systemic racism, sexism, and ableism. In her book, *Rest Is Resistance: A Manifesto,* Hersey outlines why rest is politically and spiritually urgent. She says, "Rest is a form of resistance because it disrupts and pushes back against capitalism and white supremacy. Both these toxic systems refuse to see the inherent divinity in human beings and have used bodies as a tool for production, evil, and destruction for centuries. Grind culture has made us all human machines, willing and ready to donate our lives to a capitalist system that thrives by placing profits over people."[4]

So many of us have internalized the belief that rest is a privilege to be earned. On a near-daily basis I notice myself meeting the boundaries of my energy in the early afternoon. I bargain with myself, *Have I done enough yet today to deserve a nap? Have I been productive enough to warrant a break?* Even if I do reassure myself and find my way to the couch, will I be able to enjoy a moment's peace without the reminder that my to-do list is still incomplete? Our devotion to productivity makes it hard to listen to the signals our bodies send us. When social media insinuates that "lazy" is the dialectical alternative to "productive," how can we believe that we have truly done "enough" to deserve rest?

The concept of laziness has a long history shaped by the colonization of North America, slavery, the religious roots of Western culture, and the ways capitalism has defined our society. The etymology of the word itself refers to a quality of being weak, fragile, decrepit, and immoral.[5] *Laziness* carries the connotation that a person is morally corrupt if they are unable or unwilling to work at our culture's increasingly unattainable benchmark of productivity.

In *Laziness Does Not Exist*, author Devon Price, PhD, describes the treadmill we often find ourselves handcuffed to. "No level of success grants a person the social permission to stop and catch their breath. We're forever left wondering *What's next? What else?* The Laziness Lie teaches that the harder you work, the better a person you are, but it never actually defines what an acceptable level of 'hard' might look like."[6] Social media offers us increasingly extreme examples of what productivity looks like. A search for #productivity yields videos of people making salads to eat in their cubicles, Post-it note to-do lists stuck to computer screens, and coffee taken "to go" before rushing back to the grind. When we *do* see rest online, it is often framed as a reward for our martyrdom instead of something we are all innately worthy of.

Personal Histories of Laziness

How was laziness talked about in your home growing up? What beliefs were shared with you about what it means to be called *lazy*? What were the consequences of laziness? How have those messages or beliefs shifted or changed for you in adulthood?

The resistance to our culture's attitudes about laziness is what makes The Nap Ministry's performances so profound. The group organizes collective napping experiences in which people are invited to rest in public spaces. Napping together, in plain sight, participants are guided in challenging the status quo of *what* we should be doing and *when*. The people who attend these "nap-ins" don't justify their rest. They don't preemptively explain or apologize that they are resting because they woke up at 4:00 a.m. to go to the gym, met their sales quota, or have a new baby at home. The nappers demonstrate a simple and profound act of refusal: resting without a reason.

This is not simply a conversation about slowing down. Divesting from Hustle Culture involves unlearning toxic narratives around productivity and naming the systemic barriers that gate-keep wellness for all. The ability to prioritize time for relaxation and leisure requires a degree of social, emotional, and financial autonomy; it's a kind of privilege that not everyone is granted access to.

What does "quiet-quitting" mean when you work for minimum wage? What professional boundaries can you set when you're paid under the table? How do you stop hustling when your medication isn't covered by insurance? How do you justify a shift in your productivity to your boss when you're grieving a loved one?

In 2022, data from the National Low Income Housing Coalition was used to analyze the gap between the cost of living and availability of affordable housing. It found that, in San Francisco, renters would need to earn $61.50 per hour to afford a two-bedroom, market-rate apartment. The report showed that in 91 percent of US counties, a one-bedroom rental was financially out of reach for full-time, minimum-wage workers.[7]

Hyper-productivity isn't just an ideological phenomenon. For many, it's a matter of survival. Despite the prevailing bootstrap narrative, we may not have the freedom to change our immediate circumstances. In other words, America runs on hustle.

Unlinking our inherent sense of worthiness from the pursuit of productivity we see glorified on social media involves making space for the wholeness of our life and circumstances—both what is and is not within our control. We can begin to do this by:

› noticing how the media we consume impacts our ideas about what success means

> bringing awareness and action to the systemic barriers that stand between us and real rest
> creating new and personal definitions of time well spent
> generously offering ourselves rest when we need it (and also when we don't!)

My Life in Pictures

Let's start by exploring the places you already find meaning in your everyday life outside of productivity. Take five minutes to scroll through your phone's camera roll. Look for images that show the people, places, and practices that are important to you. Maybe it's a picture of a meal you made with friends, your kids, a meme your cousin sent you, or a screenshot of a text you were proud to send. Make a quick doodle that reminds you of each picture.

Six pictures that remind me of what's important in my life:

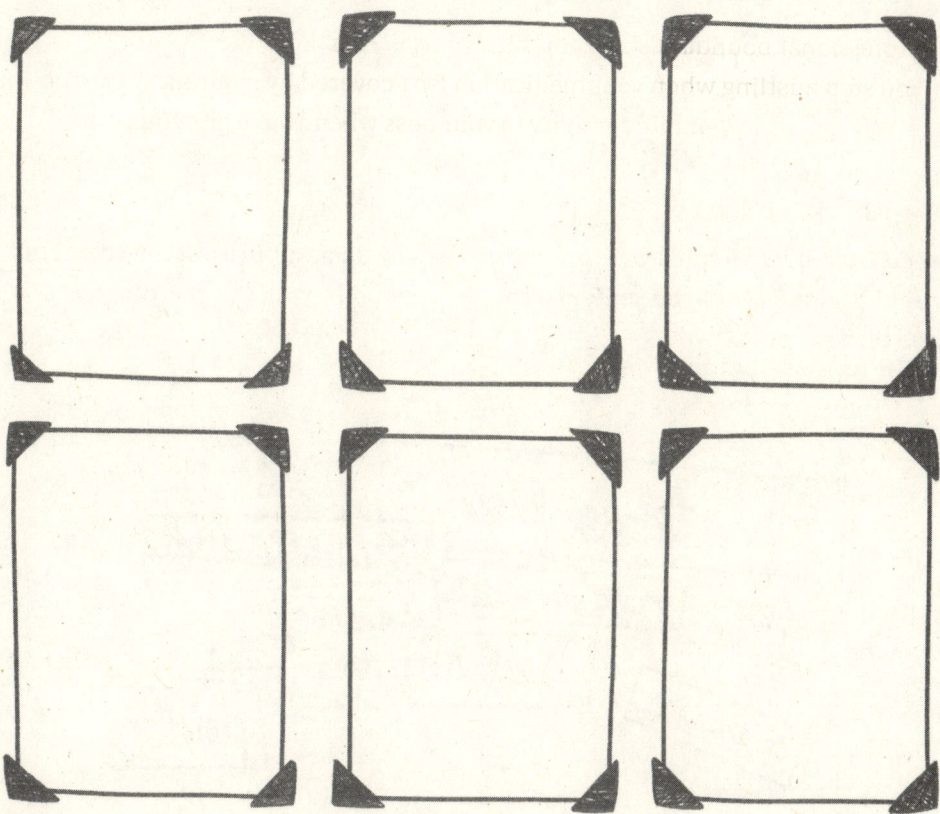

To-Do List Poem

Use this activity to deconstruct your to-do list and find the poetry within your tasks and responsibilities.

Step 1

On the opposite page, write out your to-do list.

Step 2

Now that you've created your to-do list, pause. What emotions or sensations do you notice? How did it feel to turn your attention to the tasks on your plate?

_____

_____

_____

_____

Step 3

Read back over this list and underline the words and phrases you like. This could be any part of the sentence that feels good to you. Cut out those words and phrases only.

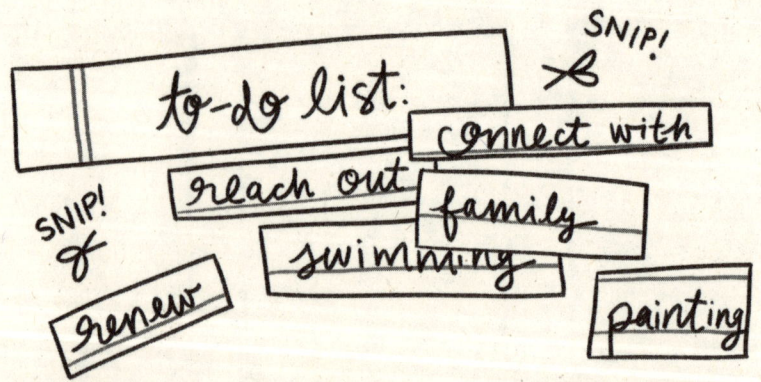

to-do list:

SNIP! SNIP!

Step 4

Find new meaning in your to-do list by rearranging the cut-out words into a poem in the space below. Feel free to change words or add new phrases and punctuation. Glue the words down when you're happy with your poem.

Step 5

How does this poem feel different from your original to-do list? What changed?

art therapist tip:

There Are No Rules in Poetry

The beautiful thing about poetry is that you don't have to follow the rules. A poem can be a list of nouns. It can be disjointed phrases, incorrect grammar, and nonsensical sounds. Your poetry doesn't need to make sense to anyone except you. Experiment with reading your poem aloud or playing with the shapes made by the negative space on the page. You get to imbue your words with meaning. You get to decide what it means and what makes sense.

Your Burnout Scale

On a cognitive level, we may understand that we are deserving of rest, but sometimes there is a dissonance between what we *know* to be true and what we feel in an embodied way. How can we allow ourselves to step aside from hyper-productivity when feelings of guilt or shame arise when we endeavor to slow down? The work (perhaps an ironic word choice) of re-authoring our relationship with rest begins by cultivating familiarity with our own personal signs of exhaustion and unique needs for rejuvenation.

These signals include the obvious physical signals, like struggling to keep our eyes open. In addition, our bodies, thoughts, emotions, interactions, and digital habits can also give us clues about when we are reaching the limits of our capacity or are feeling overstimulated.

The phenomenon of burnout is often misunderstood as the breaking point at which your body and mind are too exhausted and overwhelmed to continue work at a "normal" pace. We imagine it as an explosion—a point of no return, a panic attack, a health crisis, a partner's packed suitcase. But ruptures like these aren't actually burnout; they are its consequences.

In 1975, psychologist Herbert Freudenberger coined the term *burnout*. Its three indicators are:[8]

1. **Emotional Exhaustion:** when you feel *emotionally and physically spent.*
2. **Depersonalization:** when you have *trouble empathizing and connecting with others.*
3. **Decreased Sense of Accomplishment:** when *the goalposts for "enough" feel farther and farther away.*

Note: Nowhere on this list does it say *anything* about an inability to complete tasks at work or keep up appearances.

I once shared this list with a group of nurses and doctors. We laughed because, according to this definition, everyone we know is burned out. Then we stopped laughing. Burnout is not the boiling point. It's that normalized—and glorified—state of simmering with fatigue, disconnection, and perpetual hustle.

Reflect:

Who do you look up to on social media that makes burnout seem noble or worthy?

_____

_____

_____

Create Your Burnout Scale

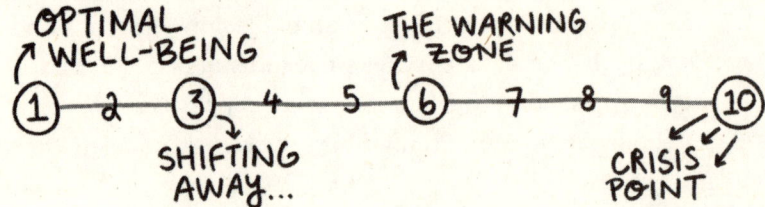

One way to care for ourselves before reaching a crisis point is to get more familiar with our spectrum of warning signs. Imagine your energy levels and emotions as a scale from 1 to 10. A 1 is the best you could possibly feel. For you, that might be a feeling of complete relaxation, contentedness, or free-flowing creativity. On the other end of the spectrum is 10, a severe mental health crisis. When we reach this end of the scale, we are often so ill or dysregulated that we need professional help to feel well again. You don't need to wait to be at a 9 or 10 to address your mental and physical health. Charting the subtle differences at various points along your scale can help you develop a sense of when you're shifting away from well-being. When we know how to recognize earlier warning signs, we have more opportunities to make adjustments to our habits, environment, and support network.

How can you tell when you are at each of these points on your emotional scale? Use the following reflection pages to brainstorm examples from your life that give you clues about your emotional and physical well-being.

Level 1

Begin by imagining yourself feeling as well as possible. Most of us don't live at a 1 all the time. This side of the spectrum isn't about perfection. Imagining yourself at a 1 doesn't mean you've been cured from all mental or physical health concerns, or that you never feel challenging emotions. Rather, it's the state of being when you have the capacity to navigate life as it is.

Example: When I am at a 1:
› The emotions/mental state I notice: *Calm, creative, enthusiastic.*
› My body feels like: *I can take full breaths easily, and my jaw is unclenched.*
› My interactions look like: *Listening with curiosity and patience, not feeling rushed in the morning.*
› My thoughts sound like: *"I have an idea I'm excited about." "I'm looking forward to seeing friends this weekend."*
› My time on social media looks like: *Putting my phone away a few hours before bed, not feeling pressure to produce content.*

When I am at a 1:

EMOTIONS:	
BODY:	
INTERACTIONS:	
THOUGHTS:	
TIME ONLINE:	

Level 3

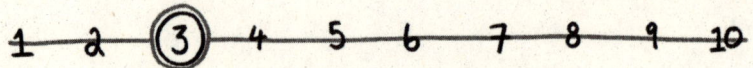

A 3 on your scale is the place where you're beginning to move away from feeling regulated. It's still safe and manageable, but things are starting to shift.

Example: When I am at a 3:

› The emotions/mental state I notice: *Scattered, slight stress.*
› My body feels: *Restless from working without breaks, knee pain from sitting in uncomfortable positions without realizing it.*
› My interactions look like: *Saying yes to more projects than I can comfortably finish.*
› My thoughts sound like: *"Have I done enough today?" "How long until the weekend?"*
› My time on social media looks like: *Scrolling to procrastinate another task, feeling jealous of people posting vacation pictures.*

When I am at a 3:

EMOTIONS:	
BODY:	
INTERACTIONS:	
THOUGHTS:	
TIME ONLINE:	

Level 6

The reason we're focusing on 6 instead of 8 or 9 is because there is still some distance from the danger zone of total burnout. A 6 might be a place where you have the ability to notice that you're struggling and need to take some action to keep yourself well. A 6 is a place where you can see the warning signs and you still have the capacity to make some changes or seek support.

Example: When I am at a 6:
› The emotions/mental state I notice: *Intrusive thoughts, judgment toward myself and others.*
› My body feels: *Sleep deprived, stiff, dehydrated.*
› My interactions look like: *Telling the same frustrating story over and over, canceling plans with friends, procrastinating important tasks.*
› My thoughts sound like: *"I should feel guilty for how late I slept in." "No one understands what I'm going through." "Maybe I should fake being sick to skip work."*
› My time on social media looks like: *Staring at my phone for an hour before bed, obsessing over mean comments, leaving snarky replies.*

When I am at a 6:

EMOTIONS:	
BODY:	
INTERACTIONS:	
THOUGHTS:	
TIME ONLINE:	

Level 10

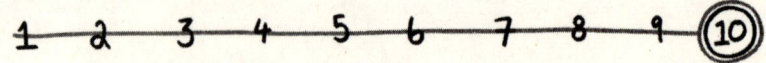

Now let's look at the extreme end of the burnout scale.

Example: When I am at a 10:
- › The emotions/mental state I notice: *Panic, fear, dissociation, extreme stress.*
- › My body feels like: *Racing heart, persistent headache, lack of appetite, back pain.*
- › My interactions look like: *Not communicating with loved ones, mold growing on dishes in the sink.*
- › My thoughts sound like: *"How did I get into this mess?" "Do I even deserve a mental health day?"*
- › My time on social media looks like: *Scrolling until early in the morning or cutting myself off from social media completely.*

When I am at a 10:

EMOTIONS:	
BODY:	
INTERACTIONS:	
THOUGHTS:	
TIME ONLINE:	

Symbolic Scale

Creativity doesn't always require art materials! We can find metaphors for our emotions and experiences in the everyday things that surround us. To make a burnout scale using symbols:

› Read back over your answers for 1, 3, 6, and 10.
› Look around your home for an object that reminds you of each of these numbers.
› Place these four objects on or near the box representing its place on the scale.
› Imagine that each object has something kind to say to you. (*Example:* "Hey! I can see you're at a 3, so remember . . .")
› Put the objects back where you found them, and allow them to continue offering you reassurance each time you notice them in your home.

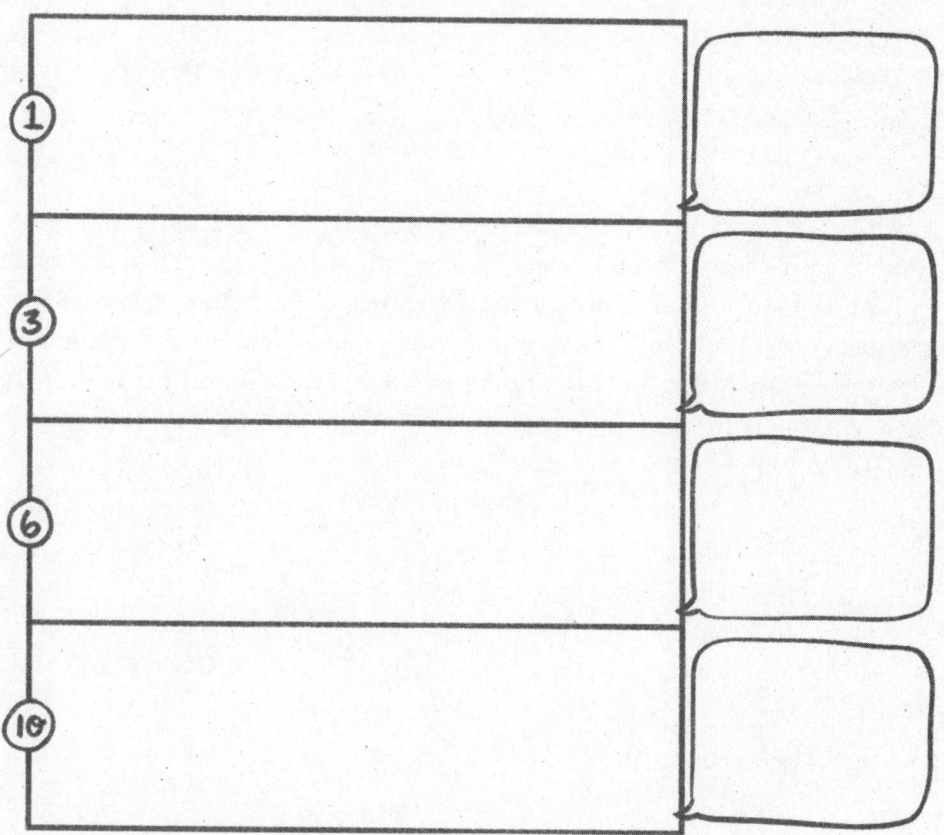

Rest Beyond Sleep

Now that you have a clearer sense of what a spectrum of capacity looks and feels like for you, let's create a personalized menu of rejuvenating acts. As you explored in your burnout scale, exhaustion isn't simply a physical experience. The same is true for rest. In a 2019 TEDx talk, physician and burnout researcher Saundra Dalton-Smith, MD, explained: "Sleep is only one part of the big picture. It's only one of the seven types of rest. Many of us are going through life thinking we have rested because we have slept, but in reality we are missing out on the other types of rest that we need. The result is a culture of high-achieving, high-producing, chronically tired, burned-out individuals."[9] In her book, *Sacred Rest*, she outlines the seven types of rest we all need for well-being. They include: [10]

› physical rest
› mental rest
› emotional rest
› social rest
› sensory rest
› creative rest
› spiritual rest

This framework helps me understand why, when I feel exhausted, I sometimes want to scroll through social media, while other times I might want to read or paint. Different practices offer us respite in different ways. If I'm craving a few minutes of screen time, it might mean that I'm tired of communicating and analyzing and I want to be passively entertained (mental rest). If I'm craving time to paint or journal, my body might be telling me that expression would feel revitalizing (creative rest).

Your Rest Menu

Take some time to brainstorm the different activities you enjoy—or can imagine enjoying—that support you in slowing down. You may have lots of ideas for some categories and just a few for others. That's not a problem. It's simply useful data about the restful activities you naturally gravitate toward.

Refer back to this menu when you need self-care inspiration.

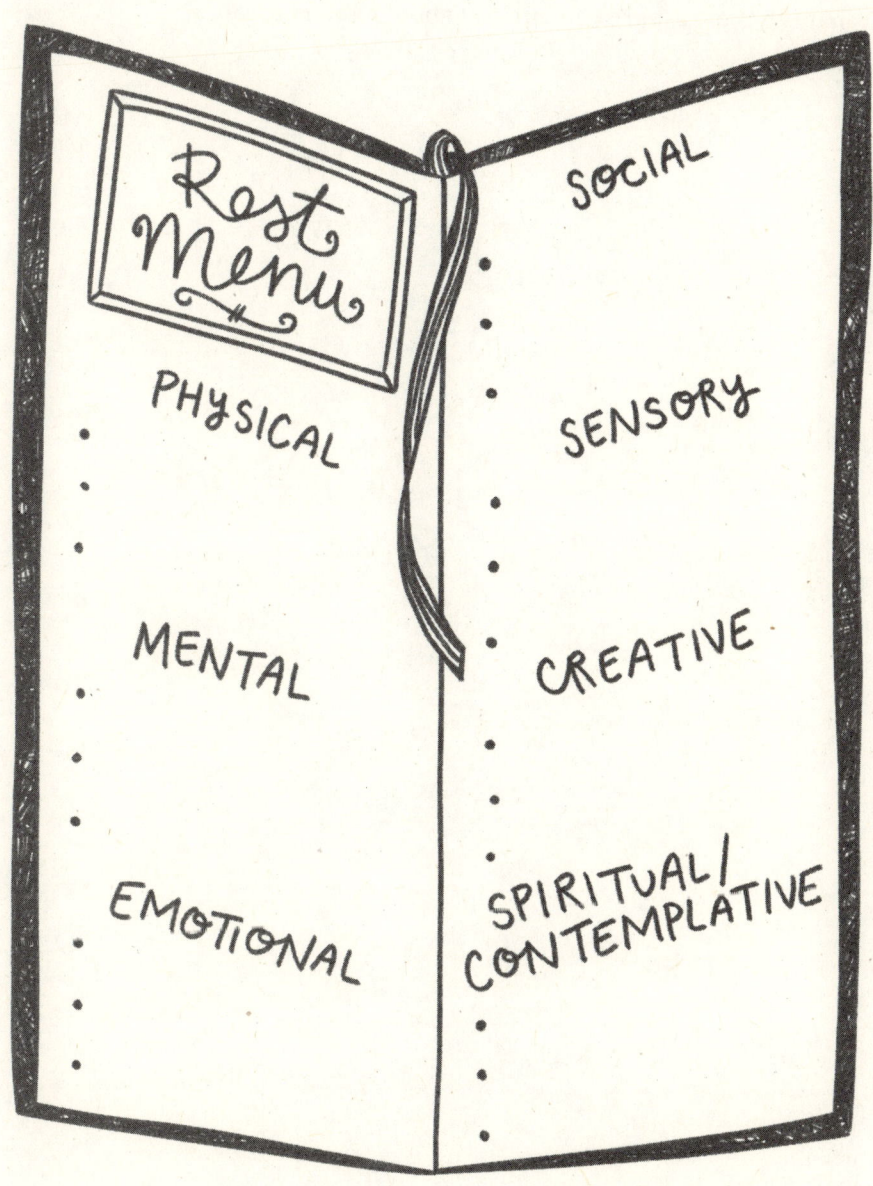

Reflect:

› After creating your menu, what do you notice about the types of rest you gravitate toward? What does that tell you about your life?
› What types of rest are you curious about exploring more?

_____
_____
_____
_____
_____
_____
_____
_____
_____
_____
_____
_____
_____
_____
_____
_____

Decision-Fatigue Fortune Teller

Making decisions can feel overwhelming when you're exhausted. Here's a tool you can reach for in moments when you want to rest but aren't sure how. Brainstorm a few different ways you can care for yourself no matter how much time you have.

› For 30 seconds, I can:

_____
_____

› For 1 minute, I can:

_____
_____

› For 5 minutes, I can:

_____
_____

› For 10 minutes, I can:

_____
_____

› For 30 minutes, I can:

_____
_____

› For 1 hour, I can:

_____

_____

› For 3 hours, I can:

_____

_____

› For 1 day, I can:

_____

_____

Choose an activity for each amount of time, and write it in the center spaces of the blank fortune teller.

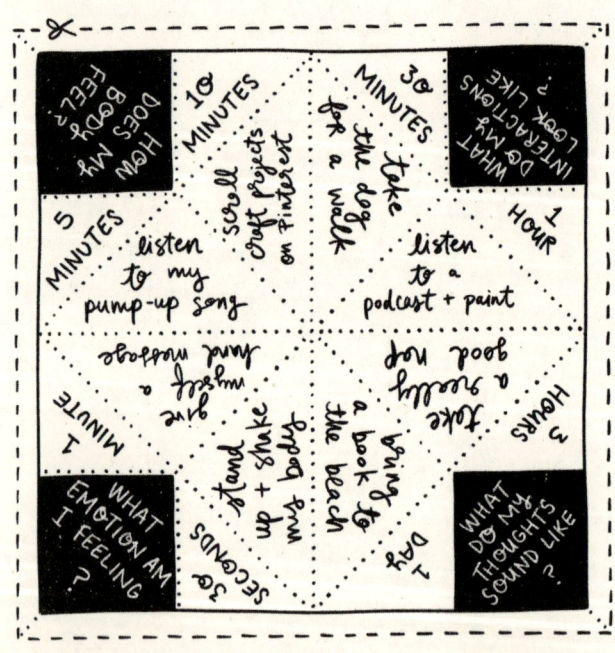

Cut out this fortune-teller template, write your self-care ideas in the center spaces, fold, and play!

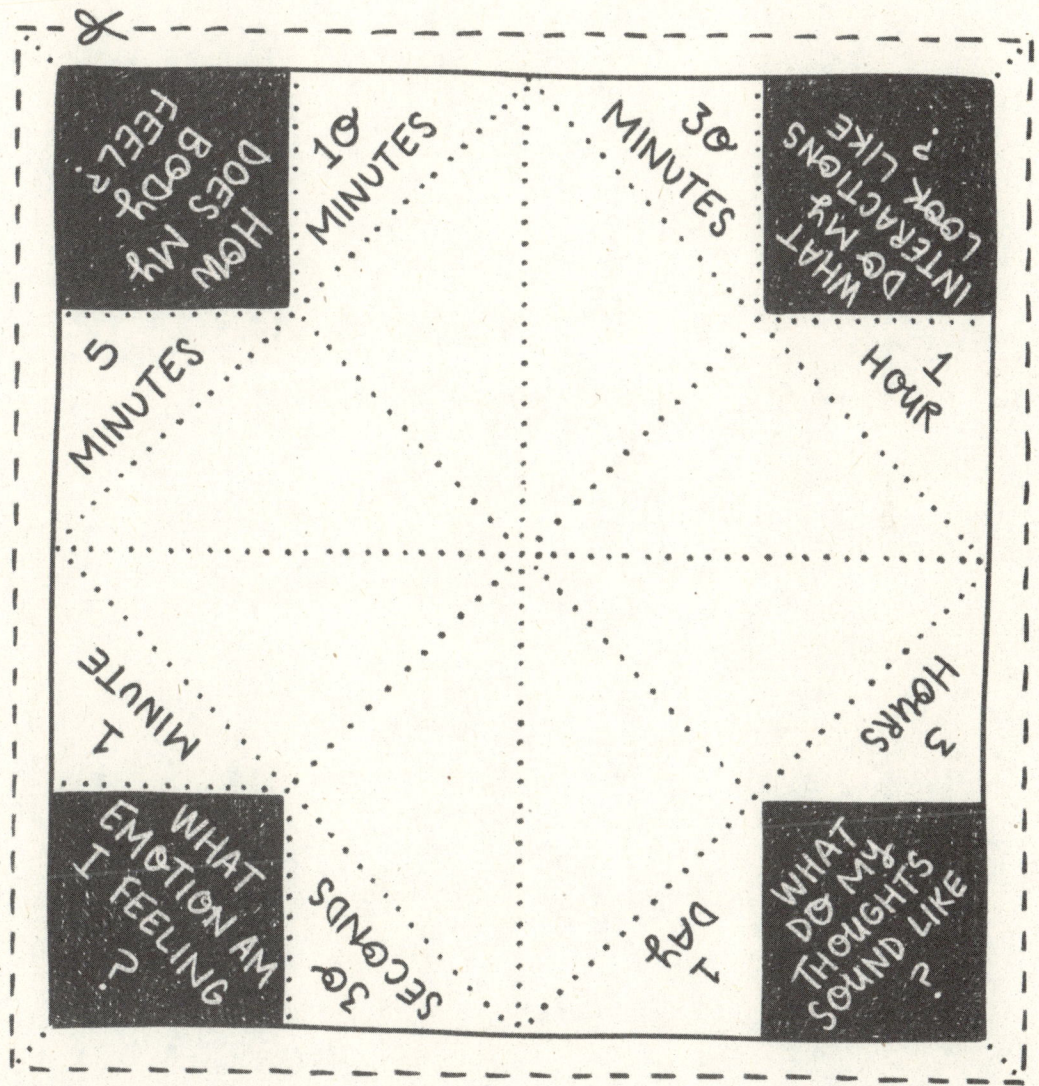

PRODUCTIVITY + URGENCY 61

- SNIP! SNIP! -

How to Use Your Self-Care Fortune Teller

1. Pick one of the four questions on the outside. Take a quiet moment to reflect on your answer while you open and close your fortune teller.
2. After your mindful moment, look at the inside of the fortune teller and choose an amount of time you'd like to take for self-care.
3. Lift the flap to reveal an idea for how you might tend to yourself. Decision made!

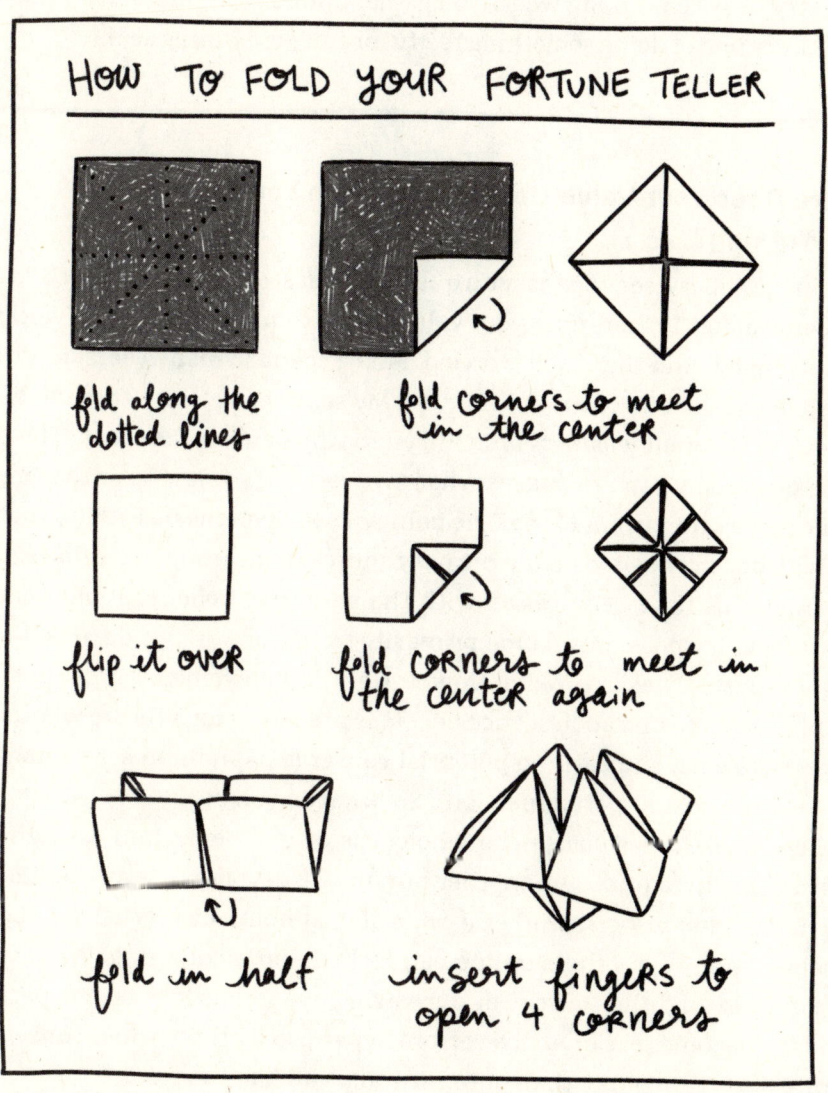

art therapist tip:

Rest Accountability Group

Accountability isn't just for tasks we deem "productive"! With friends, start an accountability group where you gather to share your intentions of resting more and to offer each other support. You could even try "lazy" coworking where you gather online or in person with the intention of doing something restful or fun—or nothing at all!

Where Does Your Value Come from When You Are Not Working?

My clinical supervisor once asked a question that stopped me in my tracks. She wondered aloud, "Where does your value come from when you're not working?" I felt stumped. And then I felt worried. I have spent so many years describing myself *as* the job I do or the field I study. My sense of accomplishment, of worthiness, of inherent *goodness* is so linked to who I am on-the-clock. The point of the question wasn't to suggest that my work isn't valuable or that my job should be less important to me. The point was to open the possibility that productivity doesn't need to be the primary source of meaning in our lives.

Many of us have been raised with the pervasive belief that our sense of identity and purpose must come primarily from the work we do. As children, we are repeatedly asked, "What do you want to be when you grow up?" The task of childhood and adolescence becomes preparing for a future where your interests, talents, and earning potential converge in an impressive answer to the dreaded cocktail-party question, "So, what do you do?"

These questions collapse the wholeness of our being into a single role, whether that be our jobs or another pursuit we devote ourselves to. I *am* an electrician. I *am* a social worker. I *am* a stay-at-home-dad. What we show of ourselves and see of others online can feel similarly confining. What would it mean to extend the sources of our value beyond our jobs or our personal brands? It becomes easier to divest from hyper-productivity when our sense of identity flows from more than one culturally validated source.

Reflect:

Instead of "What do you want to be when you grow up?," what question would you have been more excited to answer about yourself as a kid? What else would you have wanted adults to know about you and the things you enjoy?

_____
_____
_____
_____
_____
_____

Imagine you meet someone new at a party. Instead of "So, what do you do?," what question would you be more excited to answer? What else would you like to share about yourself now?

_____
_____
_____
_____
_____

Quantifying Success

We often talk about success in terms that can be easily measured:

› How much money is in my bank account?
› How many items on my to-do list have I checked off?
› How many followers do I have?
› How many accolades are listed on my résumé?

During a therapeutic-art workshop about reimagining ambition, a group member offered a reframe in the Zoom chat that forever shifted my understanding of success. Pascale Côté, the creativity coach behind the podcast *Dear Creative Mind*, suggested that instead of measuring ourselves in *key performance indicators* (a metric of evaluating performance in workplaces), we could use a framework of "key *presence* indicators." These are personal actions and signals that show we are tuned in to our values and are attending to the here and now.

Of course, presence isn't something that *needs* to be quantified and measured. Perhaps there are certain things in your life that serve as evidence of your well-being. What else could you count to measure time well spent?

For example:

› How many empty coffee mugs are beside my reading chair?
› How many poem ideas do I have in my Notes app?
› How many paint stains are on my overalls?
› How many sticks has my dog brought home from the river?

Write ideas for your own metrics of success:

› How many _____?
› How many _____?
› How many _____?
› How many _____?

Do these answers feel too easy? Amazing! Who says we need to struggle to feel good about ourselves?

Success Punch Card

Choose one of the metrics of success from the previous exercise, and make yourself a punch card. Each time you do the thing that symbolizes well-being, punch a hole or cross off a square. Cut out this card and keep it with you.

art therapist tip:

"Iffermations"

The question "Where does my value come from when I'm not working?" is a potent one that might point toward some uncomfortable feelings if you're not happy with the direction of your life at the moment. Another way to explore this topic is to imagine the possibility that something else could be true in the future. The prompts, "What if..." or "I can imagine..." open space for imagination instead of rumination on what feels uncomfortable in the present. You don't need to know exactly what should change right now. This isn't about pinpointing anything you're doing "wrong." Daydreaming about the possibility of doing something different is a creative act that can lay the groundwork for gentle change at your own pace.

Reflect:

Choose one of these prompts to reflect on:

› Where does my value come from when I am not working?
› What if I also found value in . . .
› I can imagine finding value in . . .

HACKS THAT HELP

I deleted social media off my phone. I still check it on my computer, but it feels more intentional when I have to open my laptop.

I leave my phone in my cubicle during lunch hour and eat outside.

Following social media trends and news stories is part of my job. Just saying this out loud helps me remember that being online is *work*. When I find myself drifting into research while scrolling at home, I remind myself that I'm working unpaid overtime.

I take inspiration from my Jewish community members who observe "technology Shabbat."[11] Turning off my phone on Saturdays is a way of honoring my heritage, and taking a tech sabbath is a spiritual practice for me.

I live with chronic illness. One way I manage other people's expectations of me is by setting an automatic email reply to let people know that my rhythm and pace of work are varied and that I will get back to them within a week.

I have a phone for work and a flip phone for personal use. Keeping those domains separate helps me to focus on my family.

HARVEST

@QUESTIONS_TO_HOLD_CLOSE

- How does social media impact my definition of success?

- Where does my value come from outside of work?

- What stands in the way of believing I deserve unconditional rest?

Use these activities to help you distill your reflections about how social media shapes your relationship with productivity. It might be useful to look back at your art and writing as you harvest meaning from this chapter.

Playlist: Songs for Productivity + Urgency

Take a moment to browse through music you enjoy, and pick:

› A song that helps you move at a comfortable pace

_____

_____

› A pump-up song

_____

_____

› A song that reminds you of your purpose

_____

_____

Find the Gift

Imagine your exploration of productivity and urgency has a gift for you. It might be an affirmation, a revelation, or a superpower to take with you into your future digital life. Draw it here.

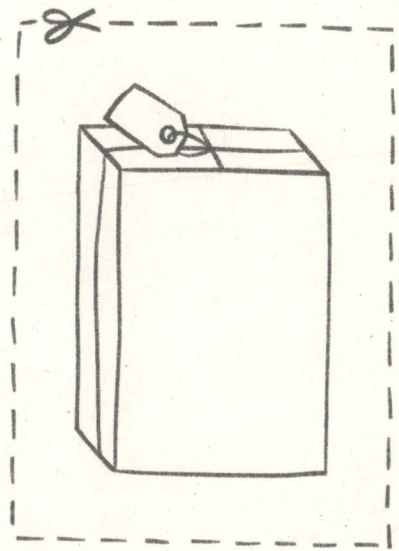

Quilt Square

Use this quilt square to experiment with pace. Color in the center square as quickly as possible with a color that reminds you of urgency. Color in the rest of the spaces as slowly as possible with a color that feels soothing.

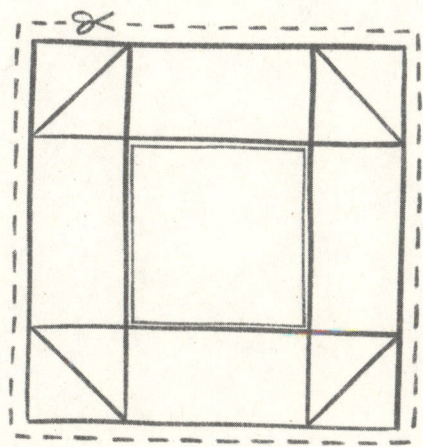

—SNIP! SNIP!—

CHAPTER 3

Privacy + Performance

#WildAndPreciousLife

The late poet Mary Oliver built her life's work around observing the natural world. She captured an intimacy with her environment in stunning and spare language, making a spiritual practice of presence with the land.

In an alternate reality, I imagine Mary Oliver forging a career in the age of social media. I picture her sitting at the edge of a pond on a wool blanket after writing something profound and disarming. She exhales and looks out over a peaceful landscape. She reopens her notebook to today's poem, then flips to a page from a few days before (her handwriting was cuter then) and artfully arranges the book to take a picture with her phone. She takes another picture with her pen lying casually across the page, then another with her travel coffee mug. In another shot, she turns the mug to hide its logo. I try to imagine Mary Oliver standing beside a pond after writing a poem and choosing a series of hashtags: #WildAndPreciousLife #LiveAuthentic #Poet #Viral.

I wonder if Mary Oliver would have succumbed to an urge to perform her presence—swiftly exiting that personal moment of union with the earth to share an update with her followers.

Vulnerability takes on a new meaning when our lives have a digital audience. Humans have answered the primal call to tell stories about ourselves since long before the advent of technologies that could disseminate information en masse. Art predates even agriculture by more than 33,500 years. It was around twelve thousand years ago that human beings began to deliberately cultivate land for crops and livestock in the Fertile Crescent region of the Middle East.[1] The earliest documented art, cave-wall drawings on Indonesia's Sulawesi Island, were created more than 45,500 years ago.[2] Even the advent of the printing press, the radio, and the television didn't carry the same immediacy and onslaught of direct feedback to the artists behind popular work as now. Today's content creators are expected not only to create work but to offer the public unrestricted access to their personal lives. I doubt Mary Oliver spent much time worrying whether her "personal brand" was relatable enough. Today, it's not just influencers carrying the burden of their followers' appetites for intimacy. It's anyone and everyone claiming a plot of attention across the digital landscape. Our innately human inclination for storytelling finds a natural home on platforms that facilitate the potential of being heard and witnessed—not just in our suffering but also in our joy, our ingenuity, our creativity.

But what happens to the boundary between a personal and public persona on apps that gamify this witnessing? What does true validation mean when your screen responds with analytics rather than eye contact? How do we behave differently when we anticipate the watchful gaze of a digital audience? How do we reconcile the connective potential of social media with the knowledge that our every move online is tracked, harvested, analyzed, and sold?

Privacy is an endangered species in the digital age.

To Share or Not to Share?

Begin your exploration of privacy by reflecting on the parts of your life that you do and don't choose to share on social media. Your decisions about what to share probably change day to day. It might depend on the platforms you use, the audiences you give access to, and how you're feeling at that moment. Use the "it depends" category to list anything in your life that can't be neatly sorted into online versus offline.

WHAT FEELS GOOD TO SHARE ONLINE:	WHAT FEELS GOOD TO KEEP PRIVATE:	IT DEPENDS:

Reflect:

Take a look at what you've written in the "it depends" category. What does it depend on? Reflect on what informs your decisions about sharing these parts of your life.

_____

_____

_____

Creators Who Make Me Feel Seen

Take five minutes to scroll through the list of people you follow on whichever platform you visit most. Which creators share about themselves in a way that makes *you* feel seen? Whose vulnerability makes you feel understood? Who do you find fascinating, wise, or helpful?

› When I see ____'s content about _____,

   I feel _____.

› When I see _____'s content about _____,

   I feel _____.

› When I see _____'s content about _____,

   I feel _____.

› When I see _____'s content about _____,

   I feel _____.

› When I see _____'s content about _____,

   I feel _____.

The Vulnerability That Makes Me Cringe

Think about a time when someone's vulnerability online gave you the "ick." What was it about that level of sharing that felt uncomfortable for you? Were you concerned for their safety? Did it feel disingenuous or overly curated? Did it remind you of something in yourself? Reflect on the way you felt in response to their sharing.

When I saw _____,

I felt _____
_____

Try stepping into that creator's shoes for a moment. What emotional need do you think that person was trying to meet by sharing? What do you imagine they were hoping to achieve with their vulnerability?

_____
_____
_____
_____
_____

CONNECTION?
SAFETY?
...
ACCEPTANCE?

VALIDATION?
REASSURANCE?
CONTROVERSY TO BOOST ENGAGEMENT?
...

On Universality

At best, vulnerable sharing creates the opportunity to dissolve stigma and foster connection. Psychiatrist Irvin D. Yalom described the importance of experiencing "universality" in the context of group therapy: "Many clients, because of their extreme social isolation, have a heightened sense of uniqueness. Their interpersonal difficulties preclude the possibility of deep intimacy . . . In the therapy group the disconfirmation of a client's feelings of uniqueness is a powerful source of relief. After hearing other group members disclose concerns similar to their own, clients report feeling more in touch with the world and describe the process as a 'welcome to the human race' experience."[3] Of course, social media platforms are not comparable to the containment, trust, and guidance offered by mental health professionals, but they can offer us glimpses into personal experiences we might otherwise believe we are isolated in.

Our daily lives may not be rich in encounters that mirror our unique outlook of the world. There is a texture of loneliness in wondering, *Does anyone else understand what I'm feeling? Has anyone else lived through something like this? Am I normal?* We often feel deeply *seen* when we witness other people share generously of themselves online, perhaps in ways that people in our face-to-face lives have never been capable of.

My most life-changing experience of universality happened on TikTok. I had spent the majority of my life wondering if I was secretly lazy, unintelligent, and inconsiderate. The effort of maintaining a facade of "having it together" seemed to take a greater toll on me than the people I surrounded myself with. It wasn't until algorithms delivered the firsthand stories of other people that I realized my shame might have an explanation: ADHD. More important, it became clear that I was not alone in harboring these secret fears about myself. It was social media that opened the gateway of my journey into understanding neurodivergence. Had it not been for strangers online sharing their stories of living with ADHD, I'm not sure if I would have found community, self-compassion, and the tools for managing life with a squiggly brain. Stigma and isolation can dissolve in the face of the universality we find on social media.

art therapist tip:

Social Media Is Not the Same Thing as Therapy

Social media can be a useful tool for education about mental health. Many of us live in countries with increasing barriers to diagnosis and professional support. Self-diagnosis can be valid and validating. That said, many mental health "disorders" share similar symptoms. For example, ADHD, anxiety, and post-traumatic stress disorder (PTSD) can present in similar ways. A trained mental health professional can offer the kind of nuanced and personalized care that you won't find in a social media post. Be cautious of one-size-fits-all advice.

Universality isn't just a matter of connection through suffering. Social media can also offer a stage to be celebrated in our pride, accomplishment, and delight. One example of the power of public joy is Jamarchay Boyd, who inadvertently started the viral #BlackMenFrolicking trend in 2022. His video begins as he records himself standing in a field of wildflowers, announcing, "I'm about to frolic!" He films himself running through the field, giggling, "Oh my god, I'm frolicking!" before lying down in the grass with a wide smile. The video, captioned with #BlackBoyJoy, received more than 3.5 million views and inspired others to make their own frolicking videos. I spoke with Jamarchay about his experience, and he explained why it felt important to share that moment of carefree delight. "You just gotta keep a good energy," he said. "This life will drain you if you allow it." His personal philosophy of positivity stands in resistance to a culture that too often portrays Black people through the lens of suffering and racist stereotypes. Jamarchay also shared his experiences of racial profiling by police and wrongful arrest. His video was filmed just days after removing a brace he'd worn for six months following a debilitating back injury. With or without the context of Jamarchay's philosophy of joy, viewers delighted in witnessing *his* delight. He added, "I love the moment. I live in it, walk in its truth, enjoy life as it comes."

When the media sees us first through the lens of a marginalized identity and tells more stories of our hardship than our happiness, a smiling selfie *is* representation. It's a way of subverting stereotypes. It's evidence for others that our identities aren't solely comprised of oppression or tokenized resilience. Showcasing our joy online can be a declaration of our multifaceted wholeness.

Megaphone of Validation

If you could stand on a soapbox with a million people listening, what validation or reassurance would you want to offer them? Write them on the lines coming out of the megaphone.

Performing Presence

I am standing in front of a truly remarkable sunset.

I'm fussing with the exposure on my phone's camera, coercing the screen to capture the impossibly vivid color of the sky. I take a few pictures and look back at my camera roll to see if the photos did the vibrancy justice. The moment is still unfolding while I scroll between images. The pink of the sunset deepens while I swipe back and forth, searching for the most compelling composition. The sky is melting into a fiery orange while I start drafting a caption, grasping for words poetic and impressive enough. The last edges of the sun are disappearing over the edge of the water. My gaze is down at the screen. Once again, I've offered my attention half-heartedly to the world around me, experiencing a sunset not with my own eyes, but through the eyes of social media.

This moment is commonplace in my life. When I look at the world through my phone, I time-travel into a near future. I leave my body and imagine I am someone else receiving a two-dimensional version of the moment I have just lived. My mind involuntarily assembles thoughts into a polished narrative to describe the scene. Fifteen years of sharing my life on social media has carved a deep neural pathway that often bypasses true presence, short-circuiting directly to copywriting in the voice of my "personal brand." Sometimes I catch myself feeling dislocated from the here and now, noticing just how enmeshed my life is with the performance of itself.

Just as art imitates life, visual trends on social media reflect the shared exhaustion of living in a state of perpetual performance. In recent years, digital trends have shifted away from the opaquely premeditated feeds that were once the status quo. As video-based platforms outpace apps prioritizing still images, we've witnessed a rise in visual signifiers of "authenticity": blurry photos without filters or Facetune, shaky videos with hasty editing, and glimpses behind the scenes into "real life."

The comeback story of the Polaroid camera is an example of how technology and aesthetic language mirror our collective desire for deeper authenticity online. In 2008, following the commercial decline of instant cameras—in part, due to competition from smartphones—Polaroid discontinued film production and sold its factory in the Netherlands. Austrian entrepreneur Florian Kaps was distraught, commenting, "It is about the importance of analog aspects in a more and more digital world."[4] By founding An Impossible Project, Kaps set out to revive the technology that allowed people to capture the moment in an accessible and tactile way. The team fundraised to buy the factory and re-create the chemical formula of the film so that people could continue using their Polaroid cameras. The project was a success and acquired the name Polaroid Originals in 2017. Today, the newest models of Polaroids come with an app that allows you to integrate your camera with your smartphone. You can have your presence and post it too.

The death and rebirth of Polaroid film shows how our nostalgia for an analog way of life mutates in the digital age. While some use their instant film as a respite from the need to constantly engage with a smartphone, others enjoy the visuals and values associated with a time before digital photography. Neither motive is incorrect. It's simply interesting to track how visual trends follow greater societal attitudes and desires. As we yearn to step aside from the ultra-curated and controlled performance of life that often occurs on social media, the pursuit of authenticity can become a performance in and of itself—a meta-curation of nonchalance.

How can we notice when we're performing instead of really inhabiting the present moment?

I often see this internalized performance of life with new clients beginning art therapy. For many, it arrives with the panic of facing a blank page. It can be daunting to stare at an empty space with the looming pressure to create a beautiful finished piece. Clients often begin with tentative marks and keep an eraser close by. There is a fear that the lines might not add up to an impressive final product. Whether it's the watchful gaze of the inner critic or the anticipated judgment of followers, performance anxiety poisons the possibility of being present and curious. The first growth edge for many art therapy clients is to unlearn the habit of editing themselves in the moment. Luckily, creating art with the deliberate intention of *not* sharing or posting can help us learn to embrace intuition over outcome. Art can be a low-stakes way to practice experiencing the process instead of working toward a final product.

Bilateral Drawing: With + Without an Audience

Start by taping your workbook to a surface so it doesn't shift around as you draw. Find two pens, pencils, or crayons—one to hold in each hand. Once your work space is set up, set a timer for three minutes. Without looking at the page, spend those three minutes scribbling. It might feel right to wear a blindfold, close your eyes, or look away from the page. Simply pay attention to how it *feels* to make marks on the paper without watching the process unfold. Get curious: Do you enjoy moving fast or slow? Does it feel better to make symmetrical motions or to allow each of your hands to do something different? The goal is not to make a drawing but to have a tactile experience of playing with art materials. There is no wrong way to do this!

After three minutes, stop and look at the marks on the page.

Now try the same exercise again. Grab two drawing tools and set your timer for three minutes. This time, record a video or time-lapse of yourself drawing. Keep your eyes open, and watch your page as you fill it with scribbles. Don't worry! You don't need to post or even watch the video afterward. Just like before, the goal is not to make a drawing. Notice how this process feels different with your eyes open and camera on. What thoughts or emotions arise when you record yourself making marks?

Reflect:

How was your process different each time? How do these two drawings look different from one another? How did it feel not to see the first page as you drew? Did anything shift when you watched your art-making or when your camera watched you?

_____
_____
_____
_____
_____
_____
_____
_____
_____
_____
_____
_____
_____
_____

Bead-Making: Revealed versus Concealed

What parts of your life feel good to share and celebrate on social media? What do you prefer to explore offline, share face-to-face, or experience alone? In this activity, you'll hide words and images inside rolled paper to create beads that will be a wearable reminder of who you choose to be online versus who you choose to be offline.

Step 1

Decorate the front of each triangle with colors, words, symbols, or experiences that represent the parts of your life that feel empowering to **share online**.

Step 2

Decorate the back of each triangle with colors, words, symbols, or experiences that represent the parts of your life that feel empowering to **keep offline**.

Step 3

Cut out each triangle.

Step 4

Starting about one inch from the bottom, cover the back of each triangle with glue. Begin at the base and wrap your paper triangle around a pencil or chopstick. As you wrap, the parts of your life you prefer to keep offline will be concealed inside the bead. To keep your paper from adhering to the stick as it dries into a bead, turn it every so often.

Optional: Paint liquid glue over the outside of the bead to seal it and prevent it from unraveling.

Step 5

Once the glue is dry, remove each bead from the stick.

Step 6

String your beads onto yarn or a cord to create a wearable reminder. You could wear the beads as a necklace or bracelet, hang them from your phone case or keys, or wrap them around the doorknob of your office.

WHAT FEELS EMPOWERING TO SHARE ONLINE

PRIVACY + PERFORMANCE

WHAT FEELS EMPOWERING TO KEEP OFFLINE

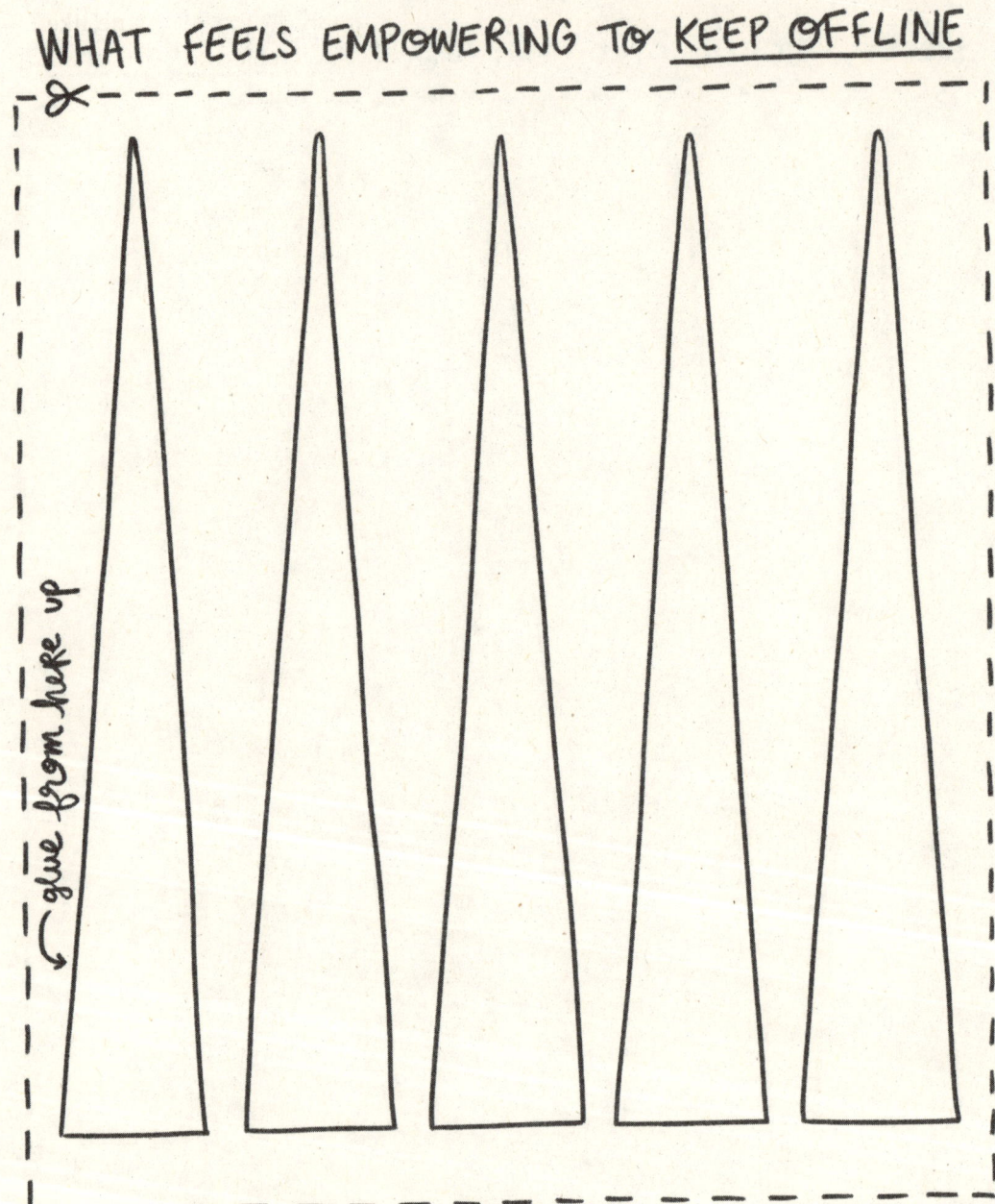

glue from here up

Romanticize the Present

Take this workbook somewhere you enjoy. It might be somewhere mundane, like your favorite seat on the bus, or somewhere with great people-watching, like a coffee shop. Or take it somewhere peaceful, like the bench at the quiet end of the park. Turn off your phone—or better yet, leave it at home—and spend some time simply observing the details around you. Be the main character of this moment, and *don't* document anything about it. Instead of making art or writing, simply exist here for a few minutes. Give yourself permission to be bored. Give yourself permission to daydream or make up stories about the people and things around you. Give yourself permission to forget what you experience. Leave whenever you're done romanticizing this moment.

☐

Are you the kind of person who is motivated by the little dopamine hit of checking a box? Go ahead + give yourself a check after this activity!

Not Telling My Trauma Story

I'm not going to tell you my trauma story.

At least, not here. Not in a thirty-second video. Not in the caption of a selfie.

Lately, I hold that piece of myself back from the edge of social media's vastness. It's not that I'm shy or that the pain is too fresh to form words around. My boundary arose from years of feeling typecast as "the girl that terrible thing happened to." I wanted other people to see me as smart, creative, or funny instead of being pinned always under the banner of "brave."

For most of my life, having a big story has been my calling card. After the bad thing happened, my story made its way through the news cycle. Sometimes it was me telling my story myself: I spoke at conferences and in classrooms, and I recounted it in every admissions essay and grant application I wrote. I also created art exhibitions about my movement through violence and forgiveness. There is no question in my mind that creativity gave me safe passage through my teens and twenties. Paintings and poems and video installations helped me to hold the hurt outside of my body and reform it into post-traumatic growth. It was my firsthand experience of healing through art that led me to pursue a career in art therapy.

But other times my story was told *for* me. When the narrative of my life was shaped by the media, it was up to journalists and producers to decide what made my story compelling. Often that meant a shocking headline and a cruel comment section. Being the subject of this type of "trauma porn" has made me incredibly sensitive to the consequences of my own vulnerability.

When we receive attention for a single facet of our identities, it's easy to feel like it is the most interesting thing we have to offer. For so many years, I internalized the message that my value was linked to my victimhood. Social media rewards hyper-vulnerability. In this way, it's possible for our suffering to become a type of social currency. It's possible to feel like we must keep retelling—and reliving—those experiences for public consumption.

The creator economy compels humans to flatten themselves or *become the niche.* We may feel reduced to a single point in a constellation of self in order to continue creating the content our audience has come to expect from us. *The photographer . . . the optimist . . . the writer . . . the mother . . . the survivor . . .* I've heard social media users wonder things like, "Will people unfollow me if I start posting about baking instead of PTSD?"

This phenomenon is amplified for those of us with marginalized identities. In order to receive acceptance, care, and advocacy, we bump into expectations that we will be visible, be vulnerable, and offer the public unfettered access to our private lives. But the result of this kind of hyper-vulnerability can be dangerous. Having a platform can also make someone into a target. In my own community, a recent drag story-time event at the local library was canceled after threats were made. When community members took the stage at a subsequent protest to advocate for LGBTQIA2S+ youth and share their lived experience, they were doxxed—their personal information and addresses shared with the goal of harassment—and began receiving violent messages from strangers online. This is, unfortunately, a common story. When we speak about the importance of representation, we also need to talk about the emotional and aesthetic labor of creating it. What personal risk is assumed by the people who step into the spotlight for the public good?

This is not to suggest that we should withhold our vulnerability or retreat into invisibility. The invitation here is to notice if and when we feel a sense of obligation to perform aspects of our identity and experience in public. The invitation includes offering ourselves permission to choose a degree of vulnerability that feels safe—knowing that we are allowed to rewrite those rules as often as feels correct. This might involve being deliberate in what we choose to share and what we choose *not* to share. This might include periods of time away from social media. This might look like the choice to leave the platforms altogether.

In their newsletter, *Monday Monday*, artist and writer Cody Cook-Parrott described the portal that privacy can create:

> In the privacy portal of no social media I find myself infinitely more free than I imagined. As I rise with the sun my mind is clear from hundreds of opinions, projects, ideas, and feelings that are not my own. I do not go on a search for signs of my inadequacy, my unlovability, or how I measure up to others. The insidious voice of doom fades away—a voice that was more persistent than I was aware of.
>
> I awake rested, hopeful, and eager to notice where I may find and attune myself to real intimacy—not the intimacy projected

onto me in a digital sphere, nor the intimacy I project that others expect of me. My portal becomes small, and I become big within it.[5]

Here is the paradox: vulnerability is liberating, and in the digital age, so is privacy.

art therapist tip:

Private ≠ Alone

Just because something doesn't feel right to post online doesn't mean you need to go through it alone. Take a moment to think about the people, pets, places, and practices that feel supportive when big emotions arise.

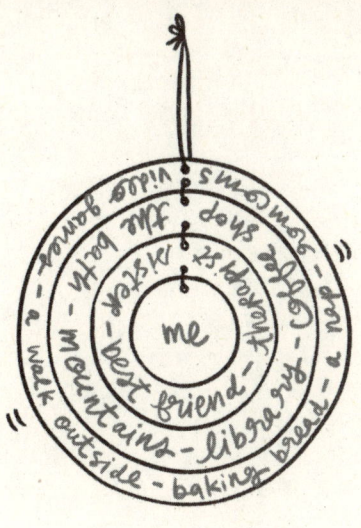

Circles of Care

Fill in the circles around you with the names, places, and practices you can turn to when you need support. When you're done, cut out your circles, punch holes in each one, use string to connect the pieces, and suspend your circles of care as a hanging mobile.

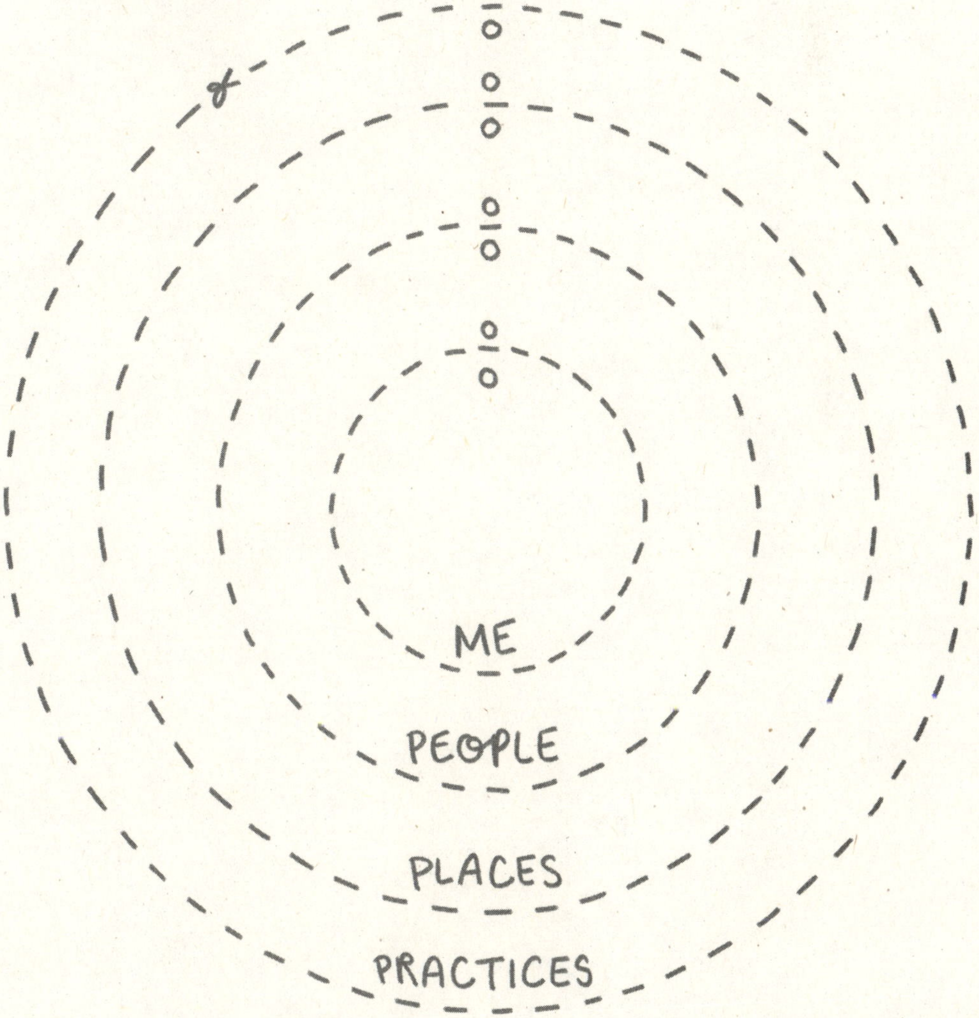

ME

PEOPLE

PLACES

PRACTICES

PRIVACY + PERFORMANCE

SNIP! SNIP!

Growing Up Online

In the digital age, we lose the ability to selectively recall the past or shape the histories other people can discover about us. It can feel like an ambush when a relic of our past is uncovered. A whole industry has emerged to solve the problem of the internet's enduring memory: services that attempt to scrub cyberspace of old photos, social media profiles, or unflattering articles. The archival capacity of digital spaces means we are reminded constantly of who we have been before.

To make matters more complex, other people also contribute to our online legacies. Each person's digital dossier is a tangled web of content created both *by* them and *about* them. In my family, the photo albums lining our basement shelves curiously end around 2008, the year a lot of us joined Facebook. Many of us reach adolescence to discover our lives already chronicled online. At an age when we're yearning for autonomy and individuation, it's jarring to realize that our personas already exist in public and that our outward identities have been sculpted by phones of friends and family. When we first sign up for social media platforms, we may use them as tools for identity formation. *How do I tell the story of myself? Is that story a new volume in the existing series, or am I authoring a new truth about myself?* A digital coming-of-age is the process of grappling with the dual autonomy and invasion of social media. We discover how public perception of ourselves can be shaped by the narratives we (or others) share, while also becoming aware of the vastness of audiences who can access our personal lives. The normal fumbling and experimenting of adolescence has higher stakes when we are watched, scrutinized, and archived by followers.

As a society, we are just beginning to grapple with the impact on children featured in their parents' highly visible social media channels. As the kids of influencers reach adulthood, many are sharing the mental health toll of having their childhoods exposed and monetized. A unique magnifying glass exists when your family's livelihood is linked to your image and personal experiences. Advocates point out that children cannot consent to the visibility and labor of influencer life. We are yet to fully understand the psychological implications of growing up "viral." How do we build a sense of identity and worthiness when we always live in a state of performance? Or when strangers feel entitled to the intimate details of your upbringing? Some states are beginning to acknowledge the potential for exploitation and explore regulations similar to the protections that exist for child actors. Currently, it's up to the discretion of parents to decide if their children's tantrums or milestones should become content.

Knowing that our past selves are preserved on social media can bring up discomfort. Our style, awareness, values, and worldview evolve over time. No one would expect you to understand the world in the same way you did when you were thirteen, yet seeing a digital relic of yourself can feel humiliating and intrusive. Whether it's the embarrassment of your middle-school LiveJournal or the trauma of being tagged by your deadname, in the digital age, it's a luxury to be forgotten.

Confidentiality Confetti

Think of a part of your life that feels important to keep private. This could be a memory, a worry, an unanswered question, or even something previously shared online that you would like to reclaim and protect. What would you express if you knew that no one else would ever see it?

Fill the space on the next page with words and drawings that will never be seen online. After you're done, cut your art into long strips. Then cut those strips into tiny squares. You've just made confetti! Throw it in the air.

Optional: Transform your expression of privacy by creating something new with your confetti pieces. Add them to your compost! Mix them into paper-mache or air-dry clay! Burn them in the fireplace and use the charcoal that remains to draw a picture! Glue them to a canvas and paint over it!

THAT'S WHY HER LEAVES ARE SO BIG — THEY'RE FULL OF SECRETS

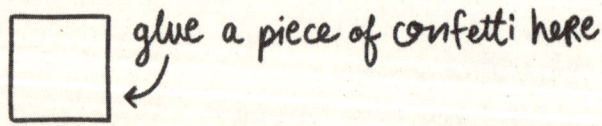

glue a piece of confetti here

CONFIDENTIALITY CONFETTI

SNIP! SNIP!

The Privacy We Don't Choose

We can make choices about how vulnerable we are on social media. We can make choices about who we follow and who follows us in return. We can make choices about which moments of life should become content and which moments should remain ephemeral, inhabited, and imperfectly preserved by memory. There is a degree of autonomy in how we approach our privacy on social media, but the amount of information you *choose* to share is minuscule compared to the volume of personal data invisibly extracted from your behavior online. Individually, we have very little control over how digital platforms track and analyze our behavior, whom that data is sold to, and how it is used.

You've probably noticed surveillance capitalism in action when advertisements in your feed seem curated to your specific lived experience. Maybe it was ads for sunscreen after you booked a vacation, health supplements after following a wellness influencer, or a therapy app after searching for divorce attorneys. The use of behavioral data goes beyond targeted marketing. In her book *The Age of Surveillance Capitalism: The Fight for a Human Future at the New Frontier of Power*, Harvard professor Shoshana Zuboff defines *surveillance capitalism* as "A new economic order that claims human experience as free raw materials for hidden, commercial practices of extraction, prediction, and sales."[6] As we scroll, these platforms build detailed avatars of our identities, preferences, habits, and beliefs. This information is valuable to those apps directly, as it allows them to customize the content we see and maximize the time we spend viewing. The personal information gathered can also be used to predict and influence our future behavior when it is sold to those with a vested interest in shaping what we see and how we act.

In 2018, the political consulting firm Cambridge Analytica was found to have gathered the unauthorized data of 87 million Facebook users to influence political campaigns, including the 2016 US presidential election. Through third-party apps, Facebook had access not just to individual users' data, but also to personal information from the people in their contact lists.[7] Former Cambridge Analytica employee and whistleblower Christopher Wylie wrote in his book *Mindf*ck: Cambridge Analytica and the Plot to Break America*: "The patterns of a social media user's likes, status updates, groups, follows, and clicks all serve as discrete clues that could accurately reveal a person's personality profile when compiled together."[8] The scandal shed light on the ways social media enables psychological profiling to deliver targeted content aimed at moving public opinion at scale.

The inverse is also true. Social media platforms have the power to expose personal information and to censor the voices of people endeavoring to communicate about injustice. The Arab Center for the Advancement of Social Media ("7amleh") documented "a dramatic increase of censorship of Palestinian political speech online"[9] following the 2021 attacks on Gaza. Social media has been a vital tool for Palestinians to organize, document instances of brutality, and denounce the violence and displacement they endure. In 2021, between May 6 and 19, 7amleh documented five hundred cases of digital-rights violations, including removing content, closing and restricting accounts, hiding hashtags, and reducing the reachability of specific content. Forty-six percent of these incidents occurred without prior warning to users, and 20 percent did not receive specific reasoning for the content restriction.[10] 7amleh continues to publish weekly digital-rights reports documenting the ongoing censorship and hate speech impacting Palestinians.

Social media platforms have a responsibility to monitor discrimination and disinformation. However, there's the potential for misuse of power when content moderation is automated, when definitions of hate speech are opaque to users, and when effective channels for reporting abuse and appealing moderation decisions are limited.

Many activists face censorship due to mistaken content violations, while others are "shadowbanned" when their accounts or content are inexplicably hidden without notice or justification. Indigenous activists in Canada have spoken out about online silencing of their advocacy. On May 5, 2021, Inuk arts and culture writer Emily Henderson woke up to messages that her Instagram stories had vanished. Emily had shared a post for the National Day of Awareness of Murdered and Missing Indigenous Women and Girls. Her peers in both Canada and the United States also posted stories on the topic that disappeared. In an interview, Emily said, "On the day when we're doing the most grieving and the most processing—and this is an incredibly heavy experience for the community—suddenly the voices, our voices, our resources, our stories are just kind of wiped without a trace or explanation."[11]

Inside the black box of the algorithm, an asymmetry of power exists between social media users and platforms. There is limited transparency about what information is shared and what is censored when our rights to privacy and free speech are mediated by for-profit companies.

So, what can we do with this information now? First, let's take some space to notice the emotions that awareness of this problem brings up:

When you think about your lack of privacy or censorship on social media, what do you feel?

_____
_____
_____

Does that feeling remind you of other experiences you've had in your life?

_____
_____
_____

art therapist tip:

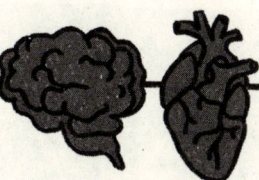

Compassion for Our Reactions

Unexpected emotional responses or "overreactions" can be important clues. It's common to have an intense reaction to a situation that reminds you of something hurtful or unresolved from the past. For example, if I am feeling outraged by learning about how my behavior is monitored online, I might start to get curious about other experiences I've had in my life when my privacy wasn't respected or I didn't have control. We can show ourselves more compassion when we notice that an old wound is being activated by a present situation.

Here is where this workbook will fall short. There isn't a journaling prompt that will prevent your phone from harvesting data about your behavior online. I don't have an art project that will grant you influence over the design of persuasive technologies. While creativity is a valuable tool in our personal healing journeys, healing also requires collective action and policy change. This is not to say that art is futile in the face of systemic injustice. I actually believe the opposite. Imagining solutions and envisioning new futures *is* a creative act. The abilities to both express ourselves and captivate others are building blocks of resistance. An art practice can help us ground and regulate when we are engaged in activism work that requires a sustained fight. Healing work is personal *and* political. Creativity can be an ally to both.

Privacy Policy Blackout Poem

Play with reversing power dynamics through poetry. A blackout poem is an easy way to change the meaning of an existing text. Below is a theoretical example of a social media platform's privacy policy—the kind most of us click "I agree" on without reading. I asked ChatGPT to read through the privacy policies of the most popular social media platforms and create an agreement inspired by the types of language they commonly use.[12]

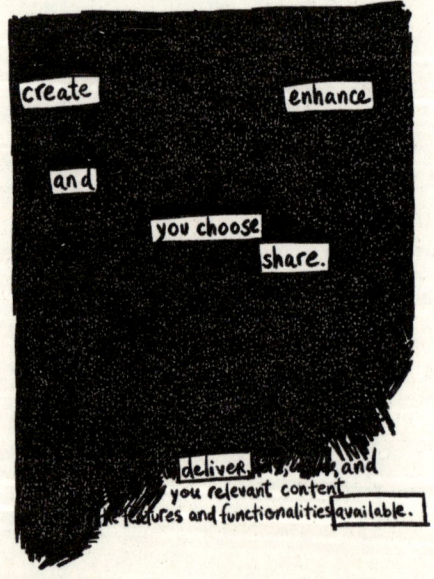

Step 1

Read through this agreement and lightly underline any words or phrases that you like. These could be phrases you find meaningful or words you simply like the sound of!

Step 2

Once you have found language that resonates with you, use a black pen to cover everything else. Place a sheet of scrap paper behind the page if your marker bleeds through. Make choices as you go about which words to keep and which to cover. Remember that your poem doesn't need to follow the rules of grammar! Once you're finished, the only words visible will be the ones you chose.

Sample Privacy Policy for Social Media Users*

INFORMATION WE COLLECT

We collect certain information about you to provide and enhance the services on this platform. The types of information we may collect include:

1.1. Account Information: When you create an account or sign up for this platform, we collect information such as your name, email address, username, and password.

1.2. Profile Information: We may collect additional information you choose to provide in your profile, such as your profile picture, bio, and any other details you voluntarily share.

1.3. Usage and Device Information: We collect information about your interactions with the platform, including the content you view, the features you use, the pages you visit, and the duration of your visits. We may also collect information about the device you use to access the platform, such as your IP address, browser type, operating system, and mobile network information.

HOW WE USE YOUR INFORMATION

We use the collected information to:

2.1. Provide and Personalize Services: We use your information to deliver, personalize, and improve your experience on the platform. This includes showing you relevant content, recommending connections or groups, and customizing the features and functionalities available to you.

2.2. Communication and Support: We may use your information to communicate with you, respond to your inquiries, and provide support regarding the platform.

2.3. Analytics and Research: We analyze the information we collect to understand and improve the effectiveness of the platform, develop new features, and conduct research to enhance user experience.

2.4. Safety and Security: We employ measures to protect the security and integrity of the platform, as well as to detect and prevent fraud, abuse, or other unauthorized activities.

HOW WE SHARE YOUR INFORMATION

We may share your information in the following circumstances:

3.1. With Third-Party Service Providers: We may engage third-party service providers to assist us in providing and improving the platform. These service providers have limited access to your information and are obligated to handle it in accordance with this Privacy Policy.

SNIP! SNIP!

3.2. Legal Compliance and Protection: We may disclose your information to comply with applicable laws, regulations, legal processes, or enforceable governmental requests. We may also share your information when necessary to protect our rights, privacy, safety, or the rights, privacy, or safety of others.

3.3. Business Transfers: In the event of a merger, acquisition, or any form of sale or transfer of some or all of our assets, your information may be transferred to the acquiring entity or entities involved in the transaction. We will notify you via email and/or a prominent notice on the platform if such a transfer occurs and becomes subject to a different privacy policy.

YOUR CHOICES AND RIGHTS

4.1. Account Settings: You can manage your account settings and preferences on the platform, including your privacy options, notification preferences, and data-sharing settings.

4.2. Access, Correction, and Deletion: You have the right to access, correct, or delete your personal information. You can exercise these rights through the account settings or by contacting us directly.

DATA RETENTION

We retain your information for as long as necessary to fulfill the purposes outlined in this Privacy Policy, unless a longer retention period is required or permitted by law. Upon termination of your account, we may retain certain information as necessary for legitimate business purposes or to comply with legal obligations.

SECURITY

We take reasonable measures to protect the security of your information, but no method of transmission or electronic storage is entirely secure. Therefore, we cannot guarantee absolute security.

CHANGES TO THIS PRIVACY POLICY

We may update this Privacy Policy from time to time to reflect changes in our practices, technology, legal requirements, or other factors.

By accessing and using the platform, you acknowledge that you have read and understood this Privacy Policy and consent to the collection, use, and sharing of your information as described herein.

*This sample privacy policy was generated by ChatGPT, which sampled language from the privacy policies of popular social media platforms in May 2023.

SNIP! SNIP!

Reflect:

What was it like to read through this example policy? What emotions or thoughts did you notice?

_____
_____
_____
_____
_____
_____

How did the meaning of this text change when you turned it into a blackout poem? What is this poem about now?

_____
_____
_____
_____
_____
_____

You Do Not Owe Social Media Anything

Conversations about privacy and vulnerability can feel tender. Even though you don't always have the ability to control the platforms you use, remember:

You do not owe social media access to your every experience.

You do not owe social media the labor of documenting and sharing your life.

You do not owe social media a perpetual performance of identity, trauma, or resilience.

You do not owe social media a consistent or predictable "personal brand."

You do not owe social media an apology or explanation when your boundaries evolve.

*You do not owe social media **anything**.*

HACKS THAT HELP

> I have hobbies that I deliberately don't share online. My woodworking is just for me!

> My spring-cleaning routine includes removing posts and tags on content I'd rather not be remembered for.

> Social media is a part of my job! That makes it easier to draw a boundary around what I do and don't post. If it's not related to my work, I keep it private.

> I give myself permission to not answer personal questions online. I don't owe anyone an answer or an explanation.

> I have two social media accounts: one is a private account just for friends and family; the second is for work. The separation helps me feel in control of who knows about my personal life.

> You don't need to feel bad about blocking or removing people! You can also limit what certain people see if you're worried about how they'll react to being unfriended.

> Our family created a Family Privacy Code. Together we agreed on things like not sharing pictures of our house and asking before posting videos of each other.

HARVEST

@QUESTIONS_TO_HOLD_CLOSE

- Where is the line between my public + private life?

- What degree of vulnerability feels empowering? How do I know when I've reached my limit?

- What boundaries feel correct today? How can I communicate if that changes?

Use these activities to help you distill your reflections about vulnerability and privacy online. It might be useful to look back at your art and writing as you harvest meaning from this chapter.

Playlist: Songs for Privacy + Performance

Take a moment to browse through music you enjoy, and pick:

› A song you listen to only when no one else can hear you

_____

_____

› A song you think other people would delight in hearing

_____

_____

› A song for when you feel like performing or romanticizing your life

_____

_____

› A song that feels like a cloak of protection wrapped around your shoulders

_____

_____

Find the Gift

Imagine your exploration of privacy and performance has a gift for you. It might be an affirmation, a revelation, or a superpower to take with you into your future digital life. Draw it here.

Quilt Square

Color the center square of this quilt block with a color or pattern that symbolizes you as your most free and authentic self. Fill the surrounding spaces to represent layers of protection.

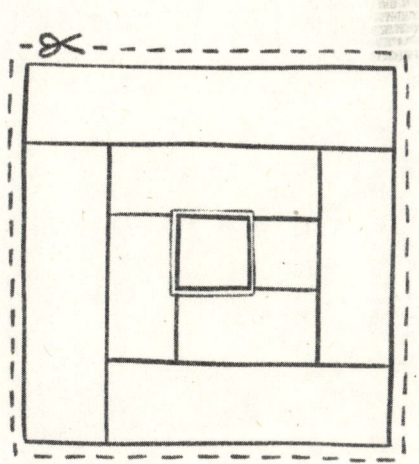

SNIP! SNIP!

CHAPTER 4

COMPARISON + WORTHINESS

Is Everyone Living Their Best Life without Me?

The everyday voyeurism of social media is a petri dish for social comparison:

She's on a literal mountaintop with her rescue dog.

They just arrived at the artist residency, and their studio has an ocean view.

He's three years sober today. His family threw him a party.

She grins, holding up her diploma. Honors distinction and a double major.

His ceramics business is really taking off. His followers are in the thousands already.

Their kids pose holding a chalkboard with "First Day of School" in perfect calligraphy.

She always comes up with the most clever and devastating reply.

It was another six-figure month, and she's got the screenshots to prove it.

They're on vacation in Europe. Again.

Is everyone living their best life without me?

    Whether a post lands like a humblebrag or a display of pride, checking social media can feel like flipping through a catalog of all the ways we don't stack up to other people. It's like the cliché of walking into a new cafeteria: You grip your lunch tray and realize everyone already has their place to sit. You scan the huge room. *Who do I see myself with? Am I smart/funny/attractive/interesting/*

121

talented/successful enough to sit with them? Am I smart/funny/attractive/ interesting/talented/successful enough to sit with myself?

Even as the culture of content evolves from an aesthetic of hyper-curation to #Authenticity, social media shows us the lives of other people at their most impressive. We *know* that a happy selfie doesn't tell a fraction of the whole story. We understand that it's not a realistic portrayal of other people's whole lives. We also know that our feeds are populated with narratives selected to make us linger, click, and purchase. Despite being aware of social media's facade, the impact of ingesting an endless stream of other people's best days and hottest takes can lead to the painful question: *What if I'm not good enough?*

As human beings, we naturally orient ourselves in society by taking stock of other people's behavior and opinions. Social Comparison Theory posits that we look to those around us to gauge our sense of worthiness.[1] Comparing ourselves to others is also how we decide which traits to emulate and which to avoid. In a pre-social media world, we might have turned to the sample groups of our classmates or colleagues for these cues. But on social media, the sample size swells to include the millions of others on platforms we use.

Let's say, for example, that I'm learning to sew. I'm not just measuring myself against the straight seams of the person beside me, my grandmother's mending chops, or the patchwork jacket in the window of my local fabric store. I'm seeing videos from a creator who was just gifted four hundred dollars' worth of damask linen, a woman who went viral for upcycling and got to quit her nine-to-five, a how-to video that makes installing a zipper fly seem *so* simple.

Contrast the slow labor of ripping the stitches out of *another* crooked hem with a fifteen-second outfit-reveal video. It's hard to feel good about myself in real time when social media presents a narrative that other people are always (or often) doing perfectly. The feeling worsens when I notice the creator's expensive sewing machine and massive fabric stash. I feel jealous of her calmness, her confidence, and her skinny arms. Anyone who has ever searched for a "beginner" tutorial can quickly find themselves feeling self-conscious about skills they arrive to the algorithm with.

Research shows that we tend to compare ourselves more harshly to the people closest to us[2]—hence, the sting of seeing your high school classmate's giant engagement ring after you've been ghosted by a Tinder date. We are more likely to compare ourselves to the people we have shared proximity with, like teammates or family members. Comparison also happens when we feel we are similar to the person on the other side of the screen. Parasocial relationships form when we experience an illusory and one-sided sense of intimacy with a stranger or character. We may feel a strong emotional connection to or resonance with another person online, despite their lack of direct interaction with us. Even if we don't know them personally, it's more common to compare ourselves to someone we see aspects of our own identity in.[3] It's human nature to measure ourselves against the people we know (or feel like we know) and the people who are similar to us.

In my own life, I notice pangs of comparison when I encounter people online who are my age and have similar qualifications, but who have *way* more followers than I do. Depending on the fluctuating frontier of my own self-esteem, I might react in very different ways. If it's a day when I'm feeling competent, cared for, and generally okay inside my life, I might look to that person with appreciation. Instead of comparing myself, I might take inspiration from their creativity or motivation from their consistency. I might even reach out to comment on how much I like their work.

But say it's a day when I'm feeling insecure: I'm lonely and wondering if I'm a bad therapist with a bad haircut who makes derivative art. I might look at that same person and see a mirror of my own shortcomings. I might wonder what I'm doing wrong and berate myself for not being better. I feel envy toward them and shame toward myself. These are both examples of upward comparison: the way we react to someone we perceive as superior to us.

Case Study of a Successful Person

A picture might be worth a thousand words, but the complexity of a life can't be captured in anything as limited as language or images. Let's try to find a deeper story than the one available online.

Find the social media profile of a person you think of as "successful." Inside this profile, draw, write, and reflect on what this person shows of themselves online.

› What does this person do really well?
› How do they demonstrate their status or value?

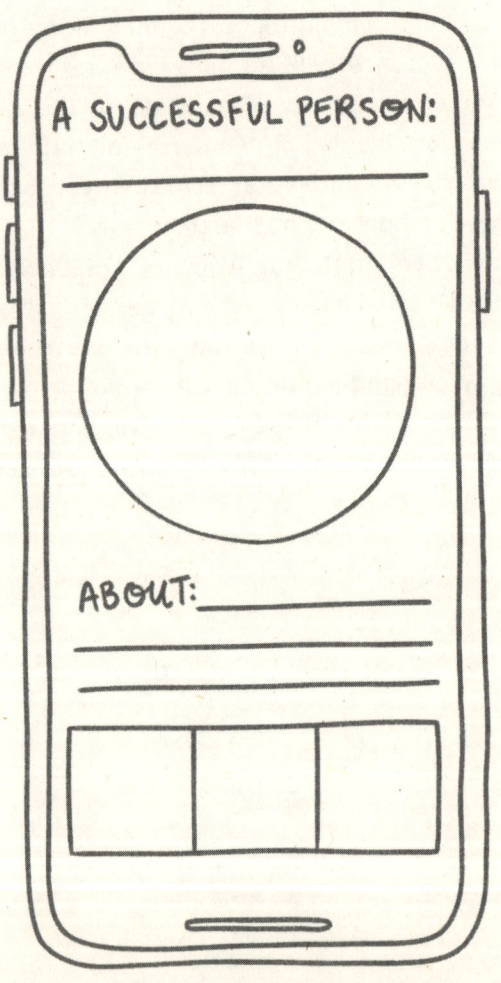

Reflect:

How do you feel about your own life when you see this person's content?

_____
_____
_____
_____
_____

What information *don't* you know about this person? You can use your imagination and make guesses.

› What parts of their life do you notice they *don't* share?
› What do you imagine they struggle with?
› What reactions do you think they hope for when they post?

_____
_____
_____
_____
_____
_____
_____
_____

"Good Enough" for Social Media

Take some time to color this page in a way that would feel "good enough" to post on social media. Don't worry—you don't actually have to share your art. While you color, imagine that your intent is to share your finished work online.

Take some time to color this same image again, but in a way that is *not* "good enough" to post on social media, whatever that means to you.

Reflect:

› What did "good enough" mean for you while you were coloring?
› What did "not good enough" mean?
› Did you notice a difference in how it felt to color each page?
› What thoughts or sensations came up while you were creating?

The Inner Well of Enough-ness

When we talk about comparison, we usually talk about the envy we feel toward "successful" people or the shame their "perfection" evokes in us. But comparison also works in the opposite direction.

Have you ever "hate-followed" someone and forwarded their videos to a friend? Perhaps you've even felt a twinge of excitement when gossip begins with *Can I be mean for a second?* If this feels familiar, you're not a monster. A moment of judgment or *schadenfreude* (delight in another's suffering) can stem from a *downward* comparison. Just as we measure ourselves against people we perceive as "superior," it's also normal to track the ways we perceive ourselves as better off than others.

Living in a hierarchical culture with limited (or hoarded) access to basic resources, it makes sense if we feel competitive with the people around us. Unworthiness can be rooted in the fear that there's not enough to go around and that our safety isn't guaranteed. The commercial definition of *beauty* is appallingly narrow. A bachelor's degree is no longer enough to be competitive in the job market. Choosing marriage and parenthood is the status quo. Our society is straight-up safer for people who are able-bodied, straight, white, and wealthy. From an early age, we are taught that our value rests in our extrinsic qualities.

It's not a personal failing if you don't easily tap into an inner well of enough-ness. The source of some feelings of unworthiness are structural. In a society that doesn't treat *all* people as inherently worthy, noticing who might be "inferior" to us offers the illusion of an advantage. Downward comparison can feel like establishing a foundation of security in a broken social ladder.

I offer this with the hope of lifting the shame of noticing that we are judging other people. It's radical to declare your inherent and unconditional worthiness *right now*. Not you ten pounds lighter. Not you when your degree is finished. Not you with a verification check mark. Getting curious about *why* we judge is the first step to interrupting a pattern we would like to change. If you would like to feel less judgmental of others, practice offering yourself compassion for being imperfect and in process.

Judgment versus Discernment

To be clear, not all negative thoughts about other people are maladaptive. Just like anger can be a signal that a boundary has been crossed, judgments can point to our inner sense of what is not safe or tolerable. Here is a question I find helpful: *Is this thought a judgment or a discernment?*

Judgment is quick. It reduces another person into their behavior and doesn't hold space for compassion. In judgment, we categorize, assume, and create divisions.

I think of discernment as an equation: evaluation + curiosity + thoughtful action + self-love. It's similar to judgment, in that it involves noticing how you react to other people's behavior. But discernment also leaves space to wonder *why* someone may be acting that way and what information is missing from the picture. From a curious place, we can make a choice about whether or not we want to engage with, participate in, or condone what we see. Discernment does not mean becoming a bystander to abuse or accepting victimization. The thoughtful-action part of this equation is where we advocate for our own needs, our own beliefs, or the safety of others. Self-love is when we offer compassion toward ourselves for the responses we have.

Example 1

Judgment: "I can't believe she would leave her dog tied up outside the grocery store in heat. She doesn't deserve to have a pet. She's a terrible person."

Discernment: "Whoa. Is that dog safe?" *[evaluation]* "I wonder if the owner is in a rush. Maybe she is preoccupied or a first-time pet owner." *[curiosity]* "I'm going to wait for a minute to see if the dog is thirsty. Then maybe I'll go inside to find the owner or an employee." *[thoughtful action]* "Animals are so important to me. It breaks my heart to worry about them." *[self-love]*

Example 2

Judgment: "Can you believe how fast they got engaged? He's so desperate that he settled for the first person to stick around. She's clueless—and probably pregnant."

Discernment: "Wow. They're engaged already." *[evaluation]* "I wonder what it feels like to be committed to someone after a few months? What does their happiness bring up for me?" *[curiosity]* "I think I need to mute their accounts." *[thoughtful action]* "I'm feeling tender seeing so many weddings online." *[self-love]*

If these examples seem exaggerated and idealized, it's because they are. To shift deeply ingrained thought patterns, we can start by noticing when they happen and gently offering ourselves alternatives. This probably won't feel genuine or seamless at first. Over time, however, discernment can become a habit we reach for more and more frequently.

> "Huh! That was a judgment! Let me try that again..."

The Roots of Judgment

I'm going to admit something unflattering about myself: I follow someone on social media whose content exasperates me. Not in a noble, social justice-y way, but in a self-righteous-Mean-Girls way. Sometimes I scroll through the content and mentally pick apart this person's line of work, their ego, and their ethics. Yet still their posts are always at the top of my feed because I reliably engage. There's a moment of almost-enjoyable anticipation when I see they've posted. *What cringey thing have they done now?*

Why do I keep following a person who brings out this side of myself? It's complicated. Is it because I really care about the work I do, and I perceive their field as having a negative impact on collective mental health? Maybe I'm annoyed that I spent three years in grad school and took on student debt to train in my profession, and it feels unfair that other people can just decide to brand themselves as "experts." Maybe I'm envious of their popularity, their body, and their affluence. My negative comparison to this person is an unconscious attempt to validate my own intelligence and seriousness. My continued engagement is a tangle of valid concerns, envy, and insecurity. When I realized I was stuck in this judgment spiral, I muted them.

What is underneath judgment? To find out, follow the path of this ecosystem to learn more about where feelings of judgment are growing from.

Log on to social media and choose a piece of content that evokes a judgmental, downward comparison.

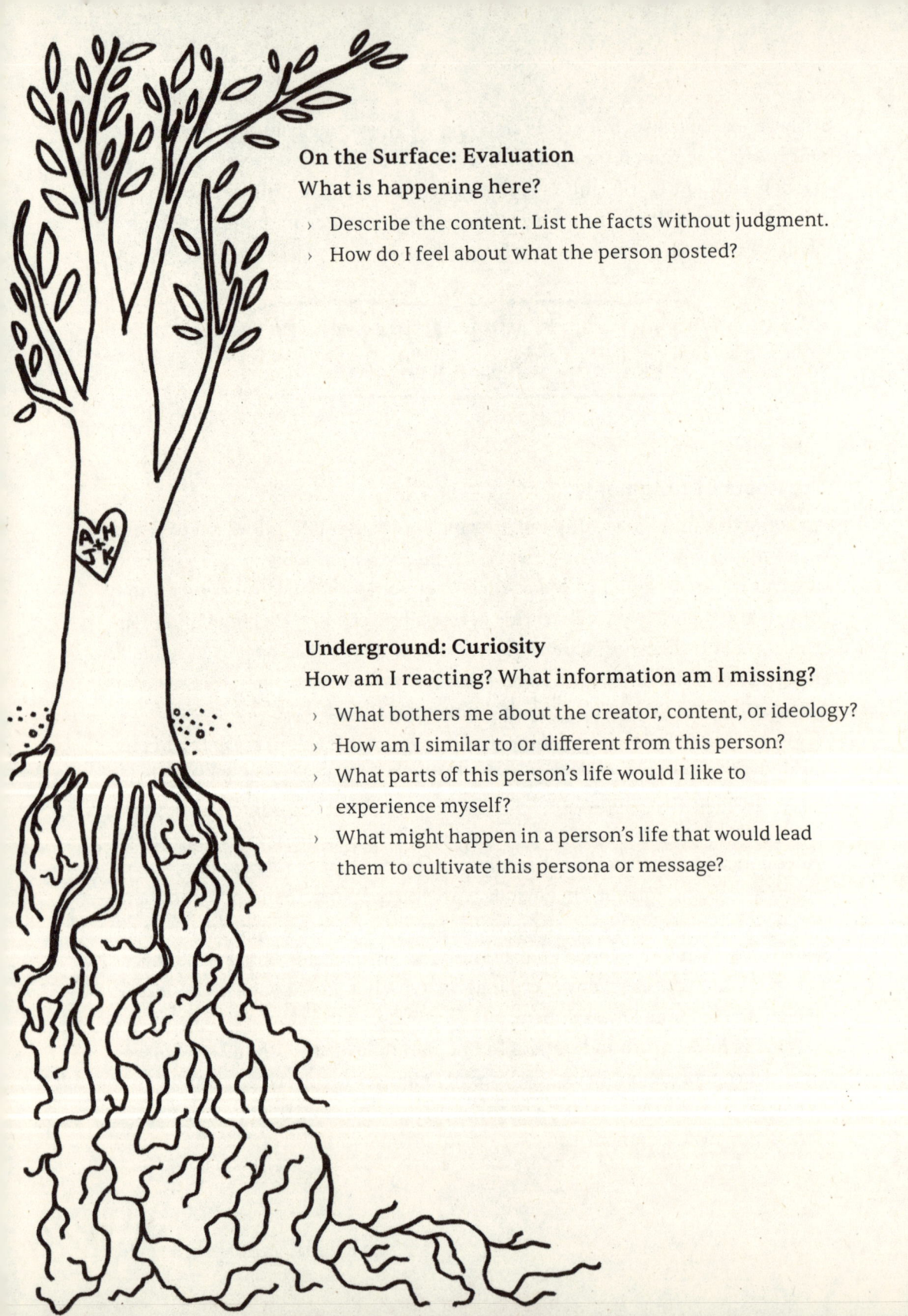

On the Surface: Evaluation

What is happening here?

› Describe the content. List the facts without judgment.
› How do I feel about what the person posted?

Underground: Curiosity

How am I reacting? What information am I missing?

› What bothers me about the creator, content, or ideology?
› How am I similar to or different from this person?
› What parts of this person's life would I like to experience myself?
› What might happen in a person's life that would lead them to cultivate this persona or message?

New Growth: Thoughtful Action
What do I want to do about it?

› Is harm being done by this content? Who am I concerned about?
› How do I need to address this judgment or discernment?
› What practical steps can I take?

Bloom: Self-Love
How can I be kind to myself?

› What do those feelings tell me about what I value?
› What reminder or validation would I like to offer myself?

Reflect:

After following this ecosystem, what did you discover at the root of your judgment?

_____

_____

_____

_____

_____

_____

_____

_____

_____

Mapping Shame in the Body

It's normal to feel shame or guilt when we notice that we're judging or comparing. In order to move beyond uncomfortable feelings, we have to first *notice* what is happening to us. Luckily, our bodies offer feedback. The sensations we feel can be important clues into what emotions our bodies are trying to move through.

My body tells me I'm experiencing shame when . . .

- racing thoughts
- tight throat
- sweaty palms
- upset stomach

Tend to the body: Ask this body what it needs. What clothing, tools, or environment could offer some relief? Draw anything that could soothe or support this body.

It's Giving Uncanny Valley

In the spring of 2023, TikTok was flooded with reaction videos. In the space of a month, sixteen million people experienced the impressive and unsettling Bold Glamour filter. Up until this point, most filters had appeared like a mask worn over the faces of users recording. If you moved quickly or waved your hand in front of you, it became obvious that your appearance had been altered. Bold Glamour behaved differently. What makes the filter unique is its use of Generative Adversarial Network technology to compare your face to a dataset of other faces. The filter edits your appearance, pixel by pixel, while you watch in real time through your camera. The result is, at once, hyper-realistic *and* completely unrealistic.

User response videos recorded the moment of surprise at seeing their appearances radically, yet seamlessly, transformed. In one reaction video, "joyful fashion" creator Hillary Kaplan laughed, "That is so surreal!" while examining her face with and without the filter's airbrushing. Her video's caption reads: "It's giving uncanny valley."[4] Many users poked and tilted their faces while trying to comprehend what they were seeing. Some reacted with amusement and began using the filter in their regular content. Others experienced a visceral discomfort seeing themselves transformed into an algorithm's subjective definition of beauty.

Hillary's comment was referring to a theory coined in 1970 by Masahiro Mori,[5] a roboticist at the Tokyo Institute of Technology. Mori's concept builds on the Freudian notion that a sense of discomfort or eeriness arises when the familiar and unfamiliar are blurred. In Mori's research on artificial intelligence, he noticed a phenomenon in which the more an object—for instance, a video-game character or a robot—resembles a human being, the more affinity we feel toward it—up to a certain point. When something appears to be *almost* human—for instance, being realistic but with subtle discrepancies—the viewer feels uneasy or even threatened by the object (think: the creepiness of a doppelgänger). The uncanny valley refers to the sudden dip in the graph plotting the humanlike realism of an object compared to our affinity toward it.

Although the Bold Glamour filter generally creates an image with angular features, smooth skin, and heavy makeup, different users' features elicit different results. For some people it feels realistic enough that the changes register as subtle, amusing, or pleasing. For others, the changes are noticeable and disconcerting for deeper reasons.

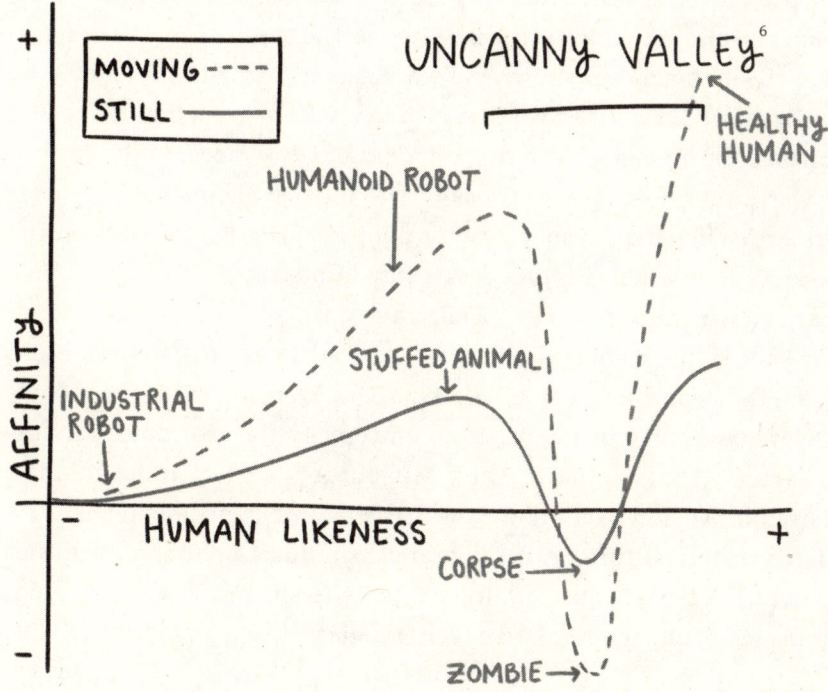

Rhona Christie pointed out another concerning possibility for Bold Glamour users. Rhona is a cancer researcher and a classically trained singer, and she often shares content about her experience of being born with a cleft lip and palate. As a person with facial differences, she was curious how the filter would interact with her features. She says: "It has taken me years to learn how to love how I look, and I really do now. I love my big nose and my unusual lips, and they really just make me who I am. But if these kinds of things [filters] had been around when I was really struggling, I don't know what it could have done to how I felt."[7]

A potentially troubling impact of this use of artificial intelligence is the comparisons we can make, not only to others, but to an unattainable version of ourselves. This technology dangles a carrot in front of us. It's one thing to see an influencer's before and after photos; it's another to make eye contact with an algorithm's "perfected" version of ourselves.

Our brains are prediction machines. We instinctively seek rules, recognize patterns, and use stimuli from the world around us to furnish our sense reality. Our sense of safety is connected to the ability to seek predictable outcomes.

A prediction error occurs when we expect to see our usual selves but instead see someone else returning our gaze—hence, the theatrics in the reveal scene of every reality makeover show. And what happens when we become familiar with a fabricated, idealized version of ourselves? What happens when a prediction error occurs looking in the mirror at our *real* faces? In the early 2000s, there was an increasing awareness of the impact Photoshop has on media consumers' self-esteem, especially for people socialized to conform to feminine beauty standards. This progress is interrupted by technologies that bring comparison to a fantasy-self just a click away.

Our skin is an ongoing artifact of passing time. Our features are inherited from the people who came before us. Our scars are evidence that we live in mortal bodies on a planet prone to entropy. In the year since I first wrote this chapter, AI tools ChatGPT and Midjourney were introduced and went mainstream. We don't yet know how artificial intelligence will shape beauty standards or the culture of media and communication, but we will need to design new road maps for attending to our self-esteem while interfacing with new and powerfully manipulative technologies.

Filter Cosplay

Two things can be true at once. Seeing ourselves through filters can feel disorienting and discouraging, *and* they can also be downright amusing. Want to see yourself as a redhead? An alien? Someone who's giving a piggyback ride to Dwayne "The Rock" Johnson? There's a filter for that!

Cosplay a character or alter ego by opening an app like TikTok, Instagram, or Snapchat that allows you to see yourself with filters on. Choose three that transport you into an identity that feels fun or empowering. How do you feel toward the person looking back at you? What character or personality do they embody? For each filter, draw a self-portrait as this new identity and reflect on each question, cosplaying as that character.

FILTER 1

Name: _____

My voice sounds like: _____

In my spare time, I like to: _____

My pet peeve: _____

I am an expert in: _____

FILTER 2

Name: _____

My voice sounds like: _____

In my spare time, I like to: _____

My pet peeve: _____

I am an expert in: _____

FILTER 3

Name: _____

My voice sounds like: _____

In my spare time, I like to: _____

My pet peeve: _____

I am an expert in: _____

Try this again with no filter! Look at yourself and reflect on the same questions.

#NO FILTER

Name: _____

My voice sounds like: _____

In my spare time, I like to: _____

My pet peeve: _____

I am an expert in: _____

Choose Your Own Lens

Imagine you're inventing a new filter. What lens would you like to see yourself and the world through?

Examples
› A filter that shows you what other people admire about you
› A filter that shows a family of ducks following you around wherever you go
› A filter that shows you surrounded by your ancestors

› A filter that _____

› A filter that _____

› A filter that _____

Nonvisual Praise

Go through your camera roll and find a picture of a young person in your life. This could be your kid, someone in your family, or a child you met in passing. Take a moment to really look at them. Think of three compliments you could give them that have *nothing* to do with the way they look.

Examples

> *You are so patient with your baby sister! I bet she really trusts you.*
> *You always teach me the funniest songs. You have a great sense of humor!*
> *That game you invented was so creative. I love it when we have time to play together.*

1. _____
2. _____
3. _____

Try doing the same thing for yourself! Find a picture of yourself in your phone or a photo album. It could be a recent photo or one of yourself as a kid. Offer yourself three compliments about something other than your appearance.

1. _____
2. _____
3. _____

Self-Comparison

My phone knows how to get me right where it hurts.

Today, I am feeling like a failure. My home is exploding with moving boxes. My knees have started aching simply from the strain of sitting cross-legged. Today is another Day One without nicotine, and I have become a grumpy collector of Day Ones. Lately, I can't seem to put myself to bed without the blue-light lullaby of one to three hours of screen time. I feel paralyzed with guilt and overwhelm. My brain shouts commands:

Instead of listening to the drill-sergeant voice in my head, I seek the passive refuge of scrolling. Maybe it was hormonal. Maybe it was the stress or the cravings. Maybe Mercury was in the microwave. But when I came across a picture of myself from six years ago, I lost my ever-living shit.

It is a selfie I took at the pool before swim practice. I am wearing a swim cap with goggles, and without a hint of irony, I am holding up both arms and flexing my biceps. I am strong and grinning with bare confidence. Looking at the selfie, I think back to that chapter of my life: I was training for a triathlon. I had just been accepted to grad school. It was an era when my phone lived in the kitchen drawer at night and I was diligent about writing my Morning Pages every single day.

Where did *she* go?

The jealousy and insecurity I feel while lurking around friends and strangers on social media pales beside the gut punch of comparing my present self to my past self. Sometimes it's the "ick" of realizing a video of my high school poetry slam still exists online. Sometimes it's the internalized fatphobia of longing for my body to look the way it did when I was twenty-four. Perhaps on a different day I might have looked at that swim-cap selfie and remembered the story differently: that I actually *hated* competitive sports and that my Morning Pages were full of reprimands and schemes to be more disciplined. Maybe I would have remembered how lonely I felt at twenty-four.

Being ambushed by my swimmer selfie reminds me of a scene from an episode of the show *Sex and the City*. Brokenhearted Carrie Bradshaw stumbles upon a picture of herself with her ex, Mr. Big. She holds the glossy photo in her hands and vows to create a rule for breakups: "Destroy all pictures where he looks sexy and you look happy."

Carrie didn't know the unique terror of being tagged in a drunken picture from a decade ago or your ex's new partner sending a "follow" request. I wonder what Carrie would write about the way phones in the 2020s create a nonconsensual slideshow of pictures of the person who dumped you—set to jaunty music.

Case Study of my Past Self

Let's try offering some compassion to a past version of ourselves.

Find something about yourself on the internet that makes you squirm. Maybe it's your old Tumblr account, a heavily filtered selfie, or something you were tagged in. For this activity, focus on a moment that feels embarrassing but still comfortable enough to reflect on. Remember that you always get to decide what feels right to explore. Imagine you are an anthropologist, studying your past self.

My cringey digital relic is: _____

Date: _____

Who created/posted it? _____

How was I or the person who posted it hoping others would react? _____
_____

Think back to this time in the past . . .

What was happening in my life? What was happening in the world around me?
_____

What was important to me then?
_____

What did I want people to know or believe about me?
_____

What was challenging for me at this time?
_____

Write yourself a love note:

Dear Past Self, I see you. I want you to know...

Case Study of My Present Self

Now let's try this again. This time, imagine decades have passed. You have grown older and inhabit your life comfortably. How might your wise, elder self understand your digital presence today?

Choose something you have put online recently. This could be a picture, a video, an article, or some other form of media. It could be something you have positive, negative, or neutral feelings about. Repeat the case study, this time imagining you are seeing the post from the perspective of your wise, elder self.

My digital relic is: _____

Date: _____

How was I hoping others would react to this? _____

As your wise, elder self, think back to this time in the past:

What was happening in my life? What was happening in the world around me?
_____

What was important to me then?
_____

What did I want people to know or believe about me?
_____

What was challenging for me at this time?
_____

> Dear Past Self,
> I <u>see</u> you. I want you to know...

Art Is the Antidote to Comparison

When it comes to comparison, we know that affect primes cognition. This means the way we feel about ourselves impacts our perceived ranking among others. Luckily, creativity is an antidote to comparison.

I notice a stark difference in my emotional state on mornings that begin with scrolling. There's a palpable anxiety that joins me through my day when I stare at a screen right after I wake up. Something that works for me is practicing "de-influenced" mornings. If I start a day with creative practices that are not informed by the news, comment sections, or who is currently going viral, there's a better chance I can actually check in with what is true for me in the moment. Even reaching for my phone to stream music or a podcast seems to steal the clarity found in silence. It's important to my mental health to have deliberate times of day when I can simply hang out with myself and my art. When I do, the barometer for "enoughness" is set by my own mind before social media opens a fire hose of opportunities for comparison and competition.

Platitudes like "You are enough" and "Know your worth" seem straightforward enough, but they rarely give directions for how we might arrive there. Authenticity and inner knowing are hard to come by when 90 percent of American adults go online daily, with 41 percent reporting that they use the internet "almost constantly."[8] How are we supposed to know where the cultural zeitgeist ends and our own truth begins? If we are influenced at every turn online, protecting time for creativity is a refuge from comparison. If comparison grows from a place of shame or insecurity, then creative practices act as scaffolding for the vines of worthiness to climb.

Art is a process of listening to ourselves and slowing down long enough to discover our own thoughts, preferences, and opinions. When we are firmly rooted in a practice of our own reflection and creation, we cultivate a sturdy sense of self. This is how *I* move a paintbrush across a page. These are the words *I* choose to express my longing and my pride. This is the way *my* body wants to meet a rhythm. Carving out offline time to express is a way to cultivate authenticity and confidence. I might not know how to survive late-stage capitalism or grieve a changing climate, but I do know how to speak my own dialect of inner knowing. It's about moving the locus of worthiness and trust from external sources to internal sources.

Protecting "de-influenced" time in your life is a way to cultivate intimacy with yourself; to discover your own measures of enough-ness; and to become fluent in the language of your own dreams, values, and perspectives.

De-Influence Your Morning

You can choose any time of day to deliberately step away from your phone to create. Whether you want to de-influence your morning, lunch break, or the hour waiting in your car while your kids play soccer, it can be helpful to have some analog activities set aside to take the decision-making out of your offline time. I keep poetry books in the bathroom as a reminder that my phone doesn't need to come *everywhere* with me. Grab a basket or box and fill it with things that will help you create comfortably.

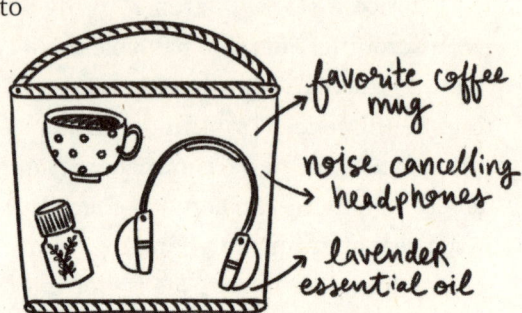

Draw the tools you gathered.

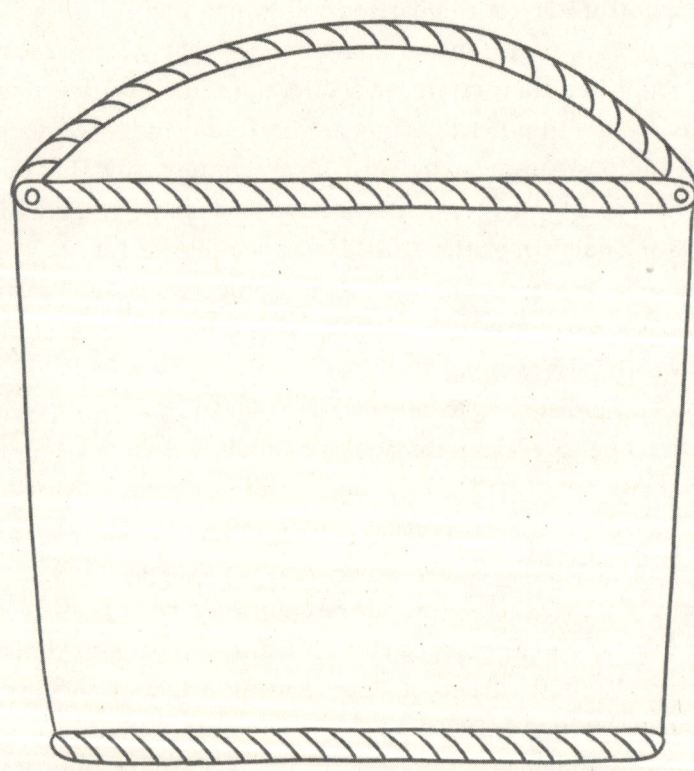

Mapping Worthiness in the Body

Just as our bodies give us clues to communicate shame, they also give us feedback when we are feeling pride, ease, and worthiness. There is so much language to describe dis-ease that we might not notice the subtle signals of positive or neutral emotions. How does your body tell you that you are feeling worthy?

My body tells me I'm experiencing worthiness when...

loose jaw, relaxed grip, even heartbeat, slow pace

Ask this body what it needs! Discomfort is not the only opportunity to listen to our bodies. What clothing, tools, or environment could protect or even emphasize this feeling of worthiness? Draw anything that could support this body.

Analog Notification Collage

Use collage images to create a phone case that sends a different kind of notification. Cut and glue words and images into the space on the next page that remind you of your worthiness. Scan and adjust your collage to fit the dimensions of your phone.

Ideas:

› Look through messages and comments on your social media accounts to find kind things people have said about you. Print or write the words to use in your collage.
› Rip out magazine pictures that remind you of qualities you admire about yourself.
› Cut out photos of people who care about you.
› Recycle an old piece of art you feel proud of and write a favorite quote or affirmation on it.

Cut out your phone case! You can seal it with packing tape and stick it to the back of your phone—or place it underneath a transparent phone case.

SNIP! SNIP!

HACKS THAT HELP

> I unfollow accounts that make me feel bad about myself. I use the mute function if it's a person whose feelings would be hurt if they discovered I unfollowed them.

> I realized that Instagram was impacting my self-esteem and contributing to my anxiety. At first, I tried deleting my account from my phone. When I noticed how much better I felt, I took the plunge and deleted my profile completely.

> When I find myself lurking someone a lot, I try to ask myself if my curiosity is coming from a place of judgment or admiration. If it's judgment, I might unfollow their account.

> When someone sends me a kind message or leaves me a compliment, I take a screenshot and save it to a folder on my phone. When I'm feeling critical of myself, I look at those images as a reminder of how other people see me.

> I set up filters to block certain hashtags. I feel better about myself when I'm not seeing as much #parenthood or #fitness content.

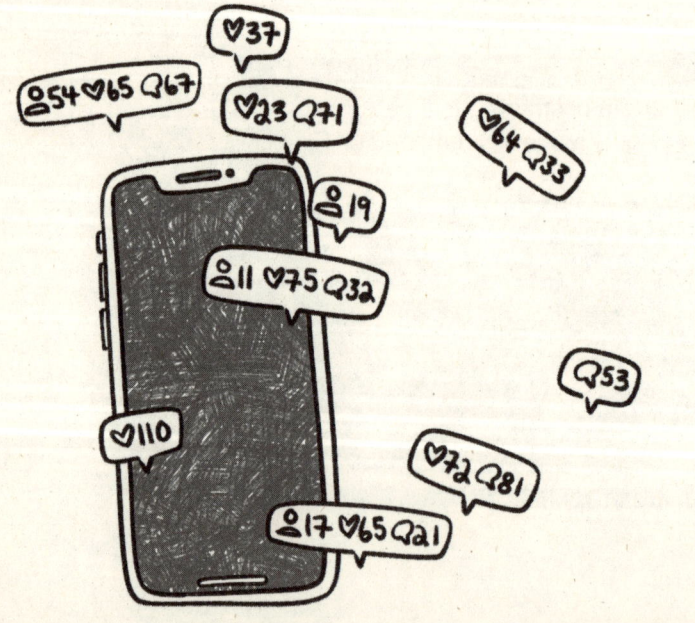

HARVEST

@QUESTIONS_TO_HOLD_CLOSE

- How do I feel about myself when I see other people's lives unfold online?

- What helps me get curious about judgments of myself + others?

- How do my mind + body tell me I'm experiencing shame? How do they tell me I'm experiencing worthiness?

Use these activities to help you distill your reflections about how social media shapes your attention. It might be useful to look back at your art and writing as you harvest meaning from this chapter.

Playlist: Songs for Comparison + Worthiness

Take a moment to browse through music you enjoy, and pick:

› A song that hypes you up when you feel "not good enough"
_____
_____

› A song that reminds you of the things you like about yourself
_____
_____

› A song that celebrates people with identities like yours
_____
_____

› A song that your body can't help but dance to
_____
_____

Find the Gift

Imagine that your exploration of comparison and worthiness has a gift for you. It might be an affirmation, a revelation, or a superpower to take with you into your future digital life. Draw it here.

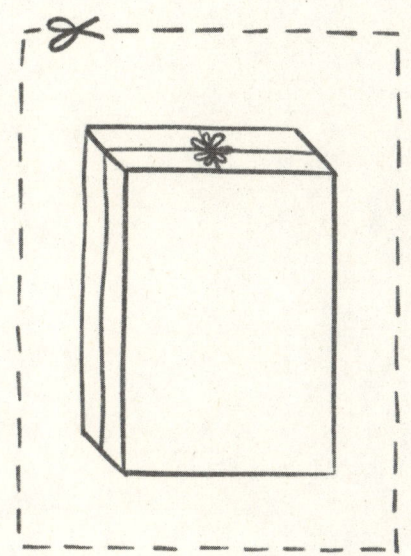

Quilt Square

Choose three colors or patterns to represent yourself at different stages of your life. Fill in the blocks on the left side of this quilt square to celebrate your past, the middle to celebrate your present, and the right to celebrate your future. What do you admire about who you were when you were younger? What do you admire about who you are today? What can you imagine admiring about yourself decades from now?

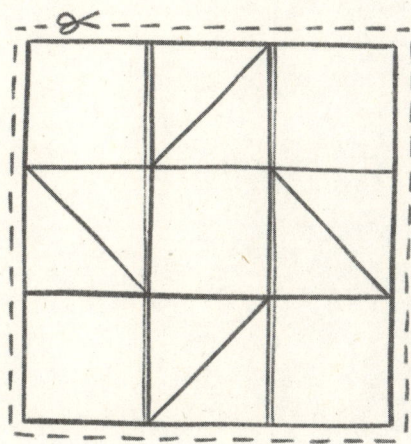

SNIP! SNIP!

Chapter 5

FEAR + ANGER + DISINFORMATION

Righteous Anger

I got into a fight with a stranger in my DMs yesterday. A man asked for my perspective on an app he was developing and took offense to my constructive feedback. He deliberately misunderstood my point and told me I was being self-righteous. I could have left the conversation alone, but instead I dug in. Between composing clever replies, I searched the pictures in his profile, looking for confirmation of the character I was painting of him in my mind. Was he materialistic? Motivated by values I detest? Did he post selfies in front of someone else's Tesla and use the hashtag #LivingTheDream? I sent screenshots of the unfolding conversation to friends who would share in my outrage and validate my stance. When I finally put down my phone, it was 11:00 p.m.—hours past the time I'd promised myself I'd log off social media. For the rest of the night, I seethed and replayed our exchange. The next day in the shower, my mind continued to rehearse the devastating responses I wished I'd sent. I repeated the anecdote of my heroic callout to anyone who would listen.

Because I am the author of this story, I get to tell you that I was right. I get to tell you that he was a jerk and I was justified in standing up for myself. Even if that's true, when I focus on the binary of right and wrong, I miss the opportunity to understand *why* I engaged in the fight in the first place.

If I am being honest, there was a part of me that found some satisfaction in the conflict. This "part" of me isn't bad or malicious; she was simply trying to get her needs met, even if the strategy she chose wasn't the most productive. In moments like this, I turn to the philosophy of Internal Family Systems (IFS), which offers that each of us have many different "parts" to help us cope with life experiences and emotional stress. Some of our parts can become burdened by experiences of vulnerability or pain. These parts may try to protect us from feeling vulnerable with behaviors such as self-criticism, self-abandonment, or heightened reactivity. Other parts are able to support us from a place of security and resilience. A core tenet of IFS is that we can work to understand and accept all of our parts, fostering a sense of harmony and integration as a whole Self. Richard C. Schwartz, the creator of IFS, explains: "When parts do take over, we don't shame them. Instead, we get curious and use the part's impulse as a trailhead to find what is driving it that needs to be healed."[1]

Perhaps my fight with the stranger activated a part of me that feels taken advantage of. I was (rightly) pissed off about how men often expect free emotional labor from women. Perhaps the fight touched a part of me that feels insecure about my intelligence, so I took an opportunity to flex. Perhaps it was the part of me that experienced violence and injustice at a young age. Maybe she stepped forward to try to advocate for me.

Curiosity is the antidote to shame. Getting to know the parts of ourselves that react and retreat can help us understand the deeper emotional landscape that shapes how we respond to ourselves and others.

Boxing Gloves

Think of a time when you engaged in conflict online. What "part" of you showed up to the fight? What do they care about? What did they want to protect you from?

Fill the boxing gloves with colors to describe this part of yourself.

Imagine yourself when you are feeling your most regulated, compassionate, and calm. What would that version of you say to the "part" that engaged in the fight? Instead of boxing gloves, what tool might they use? Draw it here.

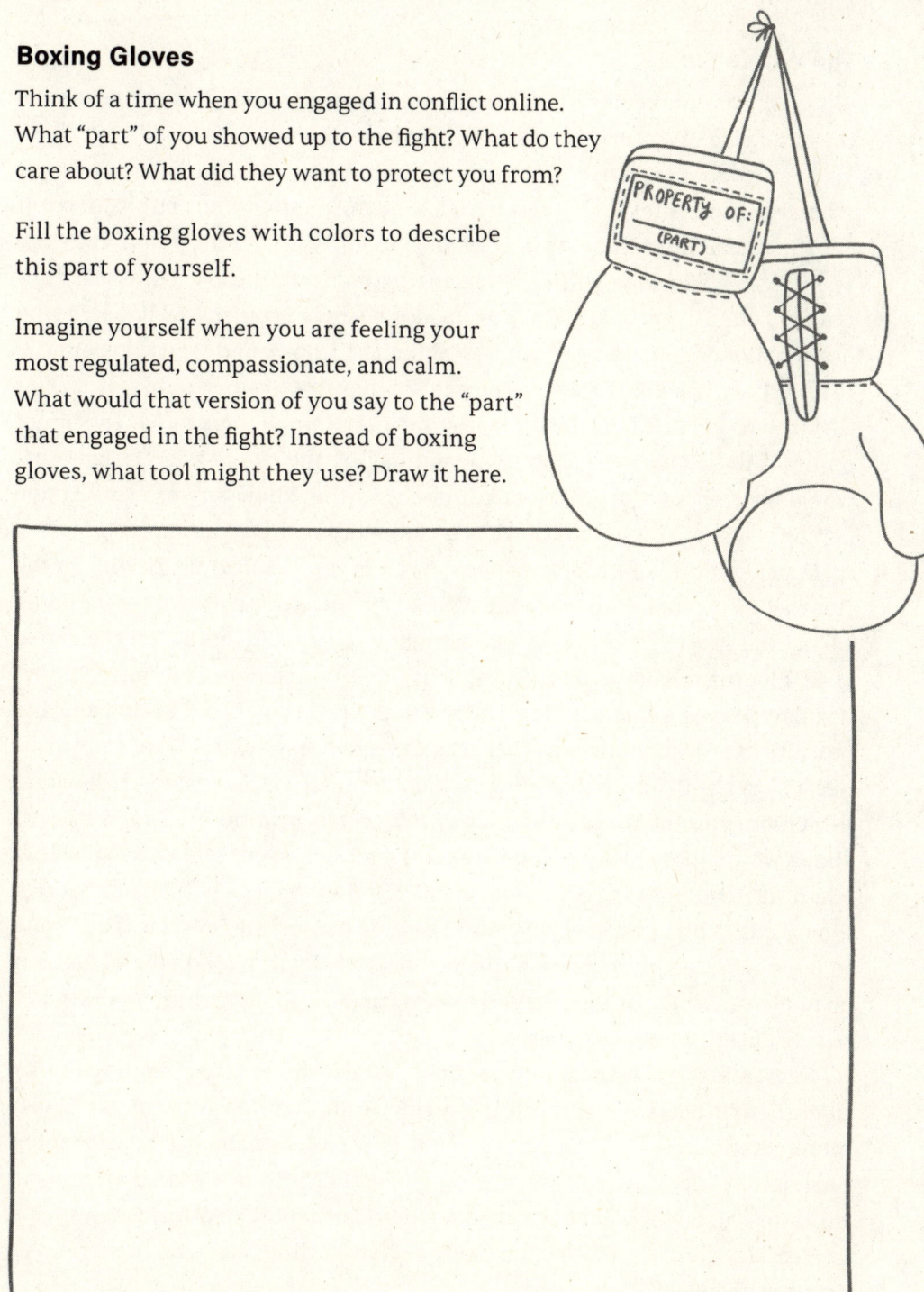

FEAR + ANGER + DISINFORMATION

The Whole Troll

When we communicate through a screen, it's tough to imagine the person on the other side of a nasty comment as a *whole person*.

Nuance doesn't thrive on social media. It's hard to respond as our highest selves in a contextual desert with a sandstorm of urgency on the horizon. Social media flattens the intricacies of humanity and, with it, our empathy. The people we engage with online can't be reduced to the cruel words they typed. Behind every avatar (bots excluded), there is a squishy-feely-being who had a childhood, feels a certain way about their boss, and worries about the future. They wonder if they are normal, if they are liked, if they matter. Our inability to hold unfaltering empathy for every single person we encounter online is not a character flaw. Can you imagine the compassion fatigue that would accompany the ability to comprehend the wholeness of every single person you share digital space with? Not to mention the vicarious trauma?

Consider how you react to someone who cuts you off while driving on the freeway, as compared to someone who walks into your path with a shopping cart at the grocery store. In my car, I might yell expletives. But in the cereal aisle, I'll probably let out an "Oops! Scuse me!" to make my presence known. (If I have PMS, I might say something slightly less Canadian.) Seeing another person's face, body, and nonverbal cues, I'm much less likely to explode. This is because of the Disinhibition Effect, which refers to the decrease in behavioral inhibition present in online and asynchronous communication. Research shows we are more likely to behave aggressively when communicating by text, when we're not making eye contact, and when we believe we can't be seen or identified.[2] While I was fighting with the rude man in my DMs, I wasn't trying to build a bridge to understand his perspective. I was pissed off and emboldened by the armor of the screen between us, so I spoke to him in a way I've never spoken to anyone in person.

Interestingly, the Disinhibition Effect is also present in positive interactions. Reddit users often admit to posting from throwaway accounts to feel more comfortable seeking advice about how to leave abusive relationships. Their anonymity is often the safest way to gather resources and plan a departure. Similarly, if speaking out loud about your mental health struggles feels impossible, the availability of text-based crisis hotlines can reduce barriers to lifesaving support.

The range of behavior fueled by toxic disinhibition exists on a spectrum. It extends from the flippant and insensitive comment sections, to unspeakable cruelty. Online, those who wish to inflict harm can easily find like-minded communities where anonymity emboldens them to express their darkest impulses. Hate is incubated on faceless servers where violent ideologies can gather momentum.

In 2014, rage and misogyny spilled over the confines of message boards, resulting in targeted violence. Women working in the video-game industry were subjected to coordinated harassment campaigns for critiquing the sexism and racism within the industry. Brianna Wu, Zoë Quinn, and Anita Sarkeesian were central targets. They were doxxed and repeatedly received violent and sexual threats. Some women who were targeted were forced to flee their homes. Amid the #Gamergate abuse, many women working in tech felt they had no choice but to leave their jobs and silence their advocacy out of fear that they and their families would be killed.[3] Online, trolls feel galvanized by their anonymity and justified in their crusades to inflict harm on others. Women and people of other marginalized identities are disproportionately targeted with abuse, with little protection from the platforms that facilitate it.

The fear and anger we express and endure online has a real impact on our well-being. Let's start by making space to hold those emotions.

art therapist tip:

Don't Rush to Empathy

You don't always need to strive toward the high road and find empathy for someone who has hurt or offended you. Anger can be a signal that a boundary was crossed or that someone's behavior is unacceptable. This is especially true when we have been victimized or oppressed systemically. We may encounter people online who completely lack empathy or deliberately engage in antisocial or abusive behavior. You don't need to extend an olive branch to someone who has just fired up their wood chipper.

Empathy is not the same thing as permission or tolerance. Similar to the distinction between judgment and discernment, working to understand another person's behavior doesn't mean we condone it or choose to endure it. It's possible to empathize with a person who is doing harm (*Wow. It's clear this person is suffering . . .*) while also holding a boundary or asking for justice and accountability (*. . . and I am going to block their account and report them*).

It can be tempting to bypass uncomfortable feelings and rush toward #GoodVibesOnly without having listened to what is bothering you. If empathy is a virtue of yours, offer it generously to yourself first. You get to arrive at empathy on your own timeline.

Permission to Be Pissed Off

Think of a mean-spirited comment you've seen online. This could be something directed at you personally, at someone you know, or at a public figure. Write the words on the banner.

Vent:

Now give yourself permission to be salty. What judgments do you have about the person who said this? What's wrong with this comment? What do the most reactive parts of you want to say in response? Go ahead. Be unhinged.

_____
_____
_____

Tend to yourself:

Take some time to reflect on *why* this comment touched a nerve for you.

› What emotion do you feel reading this comment?
› When you experience this feeling, what do you need more of?
› What do you need less of?
› Given your response to this comment, what can you tell is important to you?

_____
_____
_____

Big Feelings Box

Make a box that you imagine could hold the anger, fear, frustration, or shame you've felt when interacting with others on social media.

> Cover the inside surface of the box with a color that reminds you of this feeling. *Pause, stop, or skip this side of the box if at any point you feel overwhelmed. You never need to push yourself to explore an emotion that feels too uncomfortable.*
> On the outside, pick a color that can contain these feelings and hold them gently.
> Cut out your box, fold along the dotted lines, and tape the sides together.
> Hold your Big Feelings Box in your hands and ask yourself, *What happens next in the story of this art?* You get to decide: Does it feel right to tape this box shut to enclose the feeling? Or do you want to leave it open? Is there something you want to put inside?

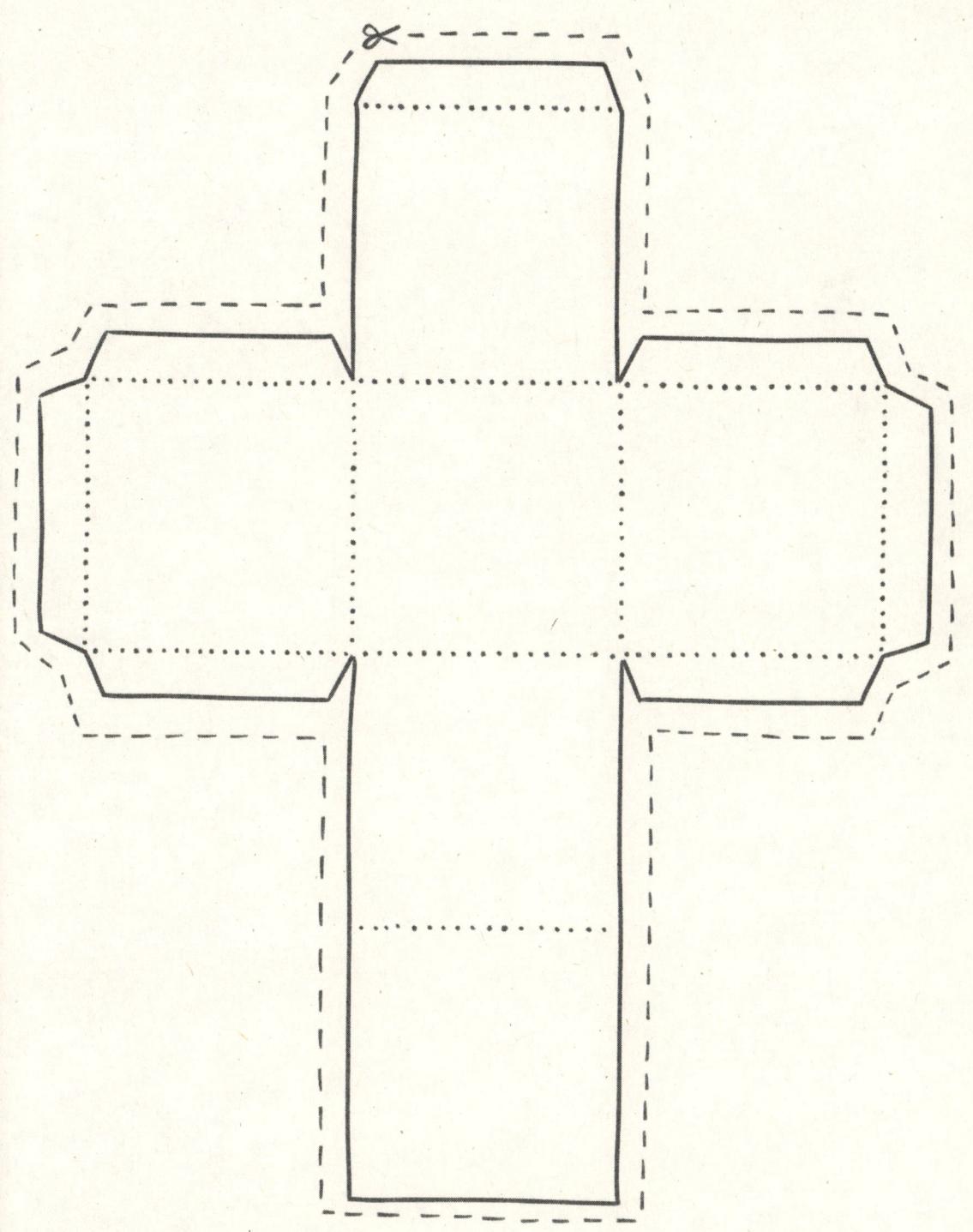

FEAR + ANGER + DISINFORMATION 169

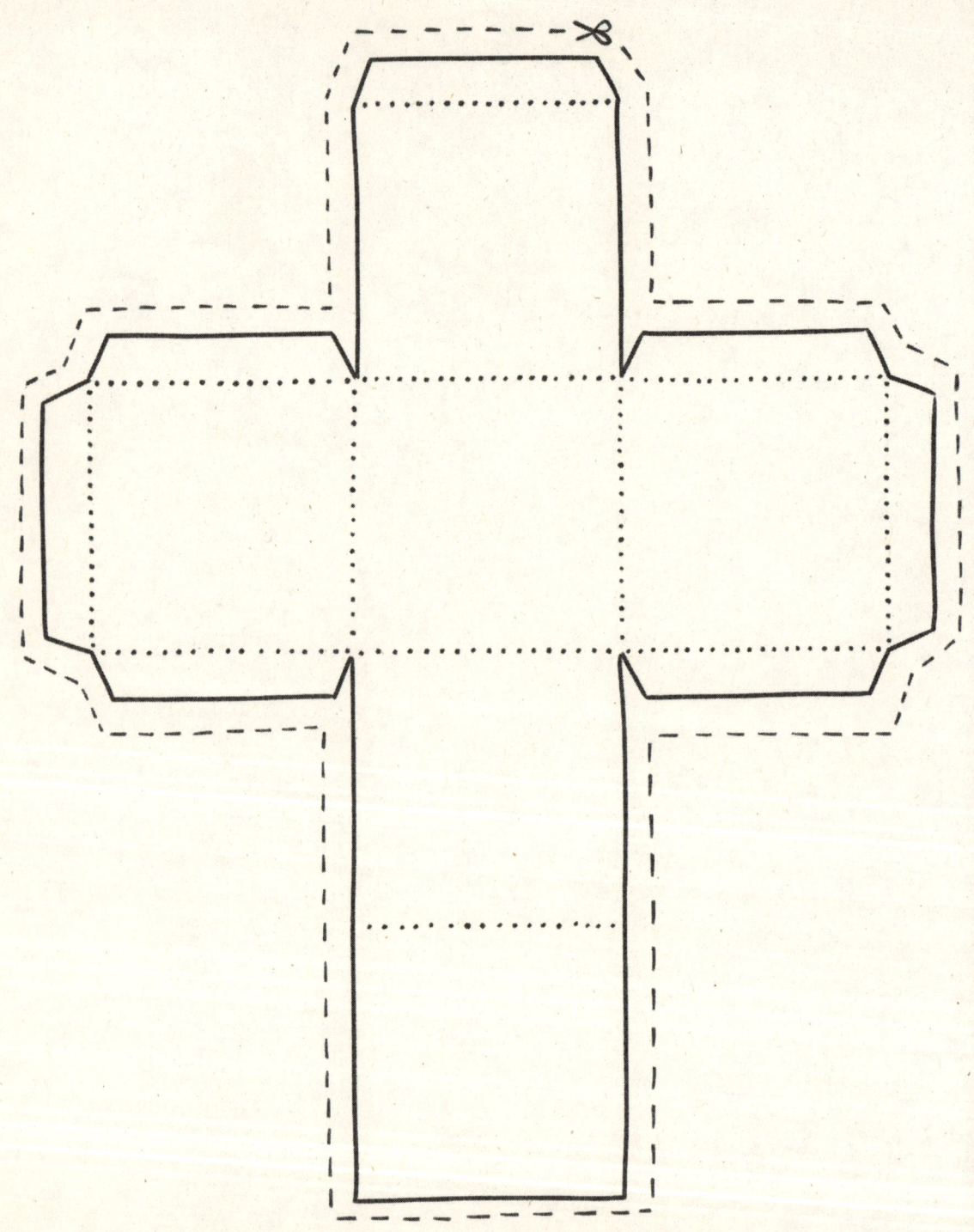

art therapist tip:

The Life Cycle of Art

A piece of art isn't finished just because you've put your materials away. What happens next is also part of the creative process. How does the meaning in this piece want to live on beyond the act of creating?

You might choose to keep your art, displaying it on the fridge or in a frame as a proud reminder. Sometimes a piece feels vulnerable and wants to be stored somewhere secure, like inside a journal or a safe. If I'm unsure what a piece means to me, I'll let it live on my desk for a few days so I can keep the conversation going.

Disposing of your art can also be a liberating option. You might want to shred, burn, or recycle it as a way of intentionally ending the process and offering yourself closure. Entropy is also a creative act.

Boundary Necklace

On social media, some boundaries are hard to define and hold for ourselves. We don't always have the ability to enforce personal rules about how others can and can't interact with us. In this activity, create a wearable boundary that you can see and feel.

› On the front side, fill the space with colors, symbols, and words that represent the types of interactions that are welcome in your life.
› On the back side, fill the space with colors, symbols, and words that represent the types of behaviors and rhetoric that you will not tolerate.
› Next, cut carefully along the lines to transform this rectangle into an unbroken loop. Wear it as a necklace, hang it from a doorknob, wrap it around your computer, or place it somewhere else you would like to surround with a metaphorical boundary.

Tip: To make this boundary more durable, you can cover the surface with a layer of packing tape before you cut!

✂⟵ - - - What is UNWELCOME - - - - cut along the lines

Disinformation: Rage within the Machine

If you used the internet during adolescence, you were probably warned by your teachers not to cite Wikipedia in research projects. Because this online encyclopedia is populated with entries written and edited by the public, the credibility of sources is inconsistent. If you were lucky, your education included discussions about assessing the accuracy of information online. Whether by accident, error, or bias, misinformation is plentiful across the internet. Today, the ability to identify trustworthy voices and discern the validity of content is a crucial skill. However, not all inaccuracies are the result of poor reporting or oversight. Disinformation is the deliberate distribution of false or misleading messages, with the intent to provoke, mislead, and influence the thoughts and behaviors of the public.

The following instances of hate, violence, and injustice share a common thread. They were perpetrated by disinhibited individuals whose actions fell under the radar of insufficient content moderation. More alarmingly, these events were fueled by conspiracies and rhetoric spread through social media. Hateful ideologies and disinformation spread rapidly to wide audiences online, aided by algorithms mandated to drive engagement as high as possible.

› In 2017, Myanmar's military used Facebook to proliferate hate speech and lies about crimes committed by the country's Rohingya Muslim minority. The resulting violence prompted a genocide and refugee crisis as 700,000 people fled to Bangladesh, where many remain displaced today.[4]

› That same year, staff and patrons fled a Washington, DC, pizza restaurant in terror when a man entered with an AR15 rifle, a revolver, and a shotgun. The gunman believed a conspiracy about a child trafficking and cannibalism ring of Democratic elites that began on 4chan, an anonymous message board. He opened fire on the door that other 4chan users had assured him would lead to the basement scene of crimes. Instead, he found a supply closet. The Pizzagate conspiracy was treated as credible news when it spread through Facebook groups, reaching millions of users and fueling outrage and disinformation ahead of the 2016 presidential election.[5]

› Riots erupted in Dublin, Ireland, during 2023, following a knife attack on a woman and three children. The hashtag #IrelandIsFull began trending as false claims spread on X (formerly known as Twitter) that the crime had been committed by an illegal immigrant. The group of far-right, anti-immigration influencers suspected of inciting the riots had been previously banned from the platform for violating hate-speech policies, but they regained access to their audiences after Elon Musk, the billionaire CEO of Tesla and SpaceX, acquired Twitter and controversially repealed content moderation protocols.[6]

If social media operates as an economy of attention, then the most valuable currencies are emotional states eliciting the highest engagement. By this, I mean not all attention is created equal. A post that sparks outrage is more compelling than humor or inspiration. A 2016 study showed that a Tweet (when Tweets were still Tweets) using "moral-emotional" language traveled twenty times farther than those without.[7] Communal judgment is a powerful force that leverages our innate drive to protect the groups we belong to and condemn injustice. The study also showed that, while these types of Tweets were more readily shared, they didn't spread far beyond like-minded groups. Not only is outrage engaging, but it is incubated within a digital echo chamber.

The tech industry's infamous motto, "move fast and break things" (coined by Meta CEO Mark Zuckerberg) propels an ethos of prioritizing rapid innovation and risk-taking. This attitude has fatal humanitarian consequences when algorithms can be easily weaponized for political and financial dominance. Moving too fast for due diligence can literally break human beings. I am not speaking in hyperbole. We have witnessed engagement-driven business models transform the ecosystem of how we communicate, how we discern "truth" from fake news, and how power is consolidated. Being exposed to outrage and disinformation on a daily basis has a profound impact on our individual mental health, and on a societal level, the cost of platforms valuing growth metrics over human life is catastrophic.

Dark Psychology

To be effective at attracting a wide and devoted audience, social media companies turn to software engineers, data analysts, and behavioral experts who can craft highly engaging—even addictive—platforms. A psychological understanding of what grips our attention, heightens our emotions, and triggers addictive behavior results in a product that ensnares its users. It's difficult to turn away from a screen that's designed to manipulate our base human instincts.

The following psychological phenomena explain why we feel so outraged and divided online—and more important, who benefits from those heightened emotional states.

What Shapes the Truth?

The ability to identify and recall danger is what keeps us alive. We are biologically primed to notice things that threaten our survival. When overstimulated, our brains naturally use *negativity bias* to filter stimuli by relevance.[8] It's hard to scan a forest for berries when an angry bear is approaching. It's difficult to concentrate on a textbook when you're waiting for your doctor to call with medical test results. You've likely seen this technique in use, such as when a creator begins a video with a shocking or unsettling hook. Whether it's "Three Signs You Have an Intestinal Parasite!" or "Your Children Are in Danger!" narratives in the media have adapted to compete in a crowded arena of increasingly inflammatory messages. Platforms direct traffic to content that engages users for as long as possible, and, in turn, creators tailor their messaging to what performs best. It makes sense that we can feel shaken after consuming a torrent of content. The culture of communication has been irrevocably shaped in the spirit of "competition at any cost."

Choose an online news outlet and spend five minutes scrolling through just the headlines. Afterward, quiz yourself. What headlines do you remember? What was the tone or emotion behind the most memorable stories?

A threat doesn't have to be personal to *feel* personal. Early primates lived in cliques. Our evolutionary drive toward tribalism is not about self-esteem or status seeking, but survival. To be ostracized is to lose the security of the collective and its resources. In turn, the impulse to cooperate and nurture a sense of shared identity feels innately protective. Because of our unconscious drive toward belonging, when an "other" (a group, individual, or idea) poses a risk to the groups we belong to, it shakes our sense of safety in the world. This is why a political debate can feel like a personal attack. *Social identity theory* is the study of how we bond ourselves to other people like us.[9] When we belong to a group that is criticized, oppressed, or otherwise endangered, a threat to the collective registers as a threat to ourselves.

Which word describes your emotions when a group you associate with wins or loses? How do you feel when your favorite sports team takes home the championship? How do you feel when your political party loses an election? How do you feel when a reality-show contestant with your same race, sexual orientation, or religion wins the prize?

The urge to protect our in-group shapes what we perceive to be true. *Identity-motivated reasoning* leads us to quickly accept or reject information depending on how it confirms or conflicts with our group identity. Our identity-based sense of truth is galvanized by the *reactance effect*, whereby exposure to alternative viewpoints can actually strengthen our opinions.[10]

I remember my response to encountering pro-life protesters for the first time. I was twelve years old and happened to be visiting the capitol buildings in Ottawa during a rally. The protesters carried posters with graphic images and statements conflating abortion with murder. Their signs and shouts didn't lead me to consider their viewpoint—it did the opposite. Even with a middle-schooler's understanding of the debate, seeing the protest made me fume and double down. I will admit that my firmly pro-choice stance didn't begin with a comprehensive knowledge of feminism or reproductive justice. It began with an almost involuntary sense that these were *not* my people. In the years since that formative moment, my politics have been shaped by research and activism, but I have no doubt that my early emotional reaction to a perceived enemy threat laid the foundation for my conviction. I don't share this to undermine my position on reproductive rights. Even if our opinions are correct, *confirmation bias* can lead us to embrace sources that validate our existing beliefs and reject information that contradicts them.[11]

 **Listen to a podcast or news clip by someone you are ideologically opposed to. Write down any statements that pique suspicion. Now listen to a host you admire speaking about the same topic. How often do you doubt the familiar voice?**

What we believe is also determined by what information we are presented with and how often those messages are repeated. *Availability heuristic* is a concept that refers to our propensity to accept messages we hear frequently because we can recall them more easily.[12] When faced with an overwhelming number of options and opinions, our brains take a shortcut, instinctively trusting what is familiar.

 **Get curious about a belief you hold or a recent decision you've made. What messages may have influenced your sense of what was true or correct?**

For example, when scanning the skin-care shelves at Sephora recently, I gravitated toward the packaging I'd seen repeatedly in my feed. The confidence I felt choosing a bottle of SPF moisturizer had nothing to do with data and everything to do with brand recognition. A more distressing example is my childhood fear of tornadoes. I must have been four years old when I saw a news segment about tornadoes on the other side of the continent. The movie *Twister* had recently debuted. Despite living in a region that had literally never experienced a tornado, the hint of a windstorm sent me into a panic. The availability of terrifying images in my child mind was no match for the facts my parents tried to reassure me with.

Reflect on what information may have unconsciously shaped your belief or choice. How pervasive was that messaging?

Truth is subjective. It is not a flaw of intellect, but a by-product of our biology that we scan our environment for threats, protect others like us, and form beliefs in the image of our emotions and social identities. This workbook is no exception. The perspectives and examples chosen are undoubtedly shaped by my biases as a leftist author and therapist. Understanding our natural biases can help us to be discerning consumers of content.

Who Benefits from Bias?

Human history is marked by divisions between groups, and the stories we tell about humanity depend on our social location. What is unique—indeed, terrifying—about this moment in history is how these innate drives can be manipulated by corporate interests to predict and influence behavior. "Perspecticide," or the extinction of free thought, occurs without our awareness or consent.

If you've ever been convinced your phone is listening in after seeing an ad appear for a product you've only ever spoken about in conversation, you've come across evidence of surveillance capitalism. Your phone microphone (probably) did not record you discussing a lime-green insulated water bottle. What actually happened was arguably creepier. Based on demographic data scraped from your profiles, your search history, your past purchases, your location, and your friends' online behavior, the algorithm made an accurate prediction. You simply noticed this one because it was eerily correct. Curating product advertisements that match your interests and aesthetics is one of the more innocent powers of surveillance capitalism. These same practices of data harvesting can be weaponized to disrupt democracy, incite violence, and corrode empathy.

As I discussed in chapter 3, Cambridge Analytica is one of the most notable instances of how unauthorized data-gathering practices can have a profound impact on the political and social landscape. The firm admitted to using data from personality tests, shared through Facebook, to build psychological profiles of American voters. Using data from social media, it was possible to identify undecided voters in swing states and target them with content tailored to their unique psychological profiles.[13] Donald Trump's digital campaign director claimed to have run 5.9 million visual Facebook ads compared to 66,000 run by Hillary Clinton's campaign.[14]

The 1998 film *The Truman Show* might be a perfect allegory for unseen influences shaping our lives. In the film, Truman Burbank is not aware that he is a reality TV star. He is filmed twenty-four hours a day, while a team of producers and actors manipulate and respond to his every action. They stage a traumatic near-drowning experience to plant a fear of water into Truman's psyche; this trauma prevents him from crossing the body of water surrounding his town—a constructed reality. In the final scene of the movie, the invisible becomes visible. His boat crashes against the edge of the TV set. Truman realizes that the horizon of his life has always been an illusion—a sky painted on the walls of an elaborate soundstage. In the digital age, the algorithmic seams holding our digital environments together are similarly imperceptible.

We can make the invisible visible by bringing awareness to the motivations provoking the outrage we feel online and the "truth" curated in our feeds. It is an act of breaking the fourth wall. We can begin to see the forest for the trees.

Observing Bias

Take some time to reflect on the worldviews, affinities, and beliefs you carry. As you reflect, notice any emotions that arise. Do you feel conviction? Protectiveness? Uncertainty?

_____

_____

Who are *your* people?

_____

_____

Who threatens the groups you belong to?

_____

_____

Which public figures do you trust without question?

_____

_____

Which public figures are you immediately skeptical of?

_____

_____

Kind Design

Design a social media platform that works differently from the usual. Imagine the features of an app that you would trust and enjoy engaging with.

What is this app used for?
_____
_____
_____

What does it show you?
_____
_____
_____

What *doesn't* it show you?
_____
_____
_____

How and when does it notify you?
_____
_____

What permission does it seek, and how?
_____
_____

Who has a say in how it operates?
_____
_____

How does it take feedback from users?
_____
_____

What kind of future does it make possible?
_____
_____

Draw the logo for your social media app here. What symbol would communicate the values of this platform?

Care + Containment in Chaos

If I am working with someone who has experienced a traumatic violation, we do not begin with watercolors. I might instead prepare a piece of paper that is secured firmly to the table with masking tape around all four sides. I'd set out pencils, crayons, or markers to draw with because they don't spill or smudge. I'd make sure the pen colors match their caps, and I'd place them on a tray. We would work in a private studio with a door that closes, where I could guarantee there would be no interruptions. The studio would be set up the same way each time they return for another session.

If my client's life has been punctuated by a lack of control and mistrust, I prepare the space and materials in a way that is deliberately predictable and contained. A wide tape border around a piece of paper cannot undo past harm, but it can prevent the page from shifting suddenly. That tape boundary visually defines a space where something new might emerge. Over time, that client may come to trust that paper can reliably hold their expressions and that they, in turn, know how to hold themselves through art. Containment can create a foundation for safety.

The internet is the antithesis of containment.

Just as the human brain struggles to comprehend the vastness of outer space, the imperceptible, evolving makeup of the digital realm can create a sort of psychic vertigo. It's hard to get our bearings on terrain that can't be mapped. We are faced with a conundrum when we try to cultivate a sense of safety in a place that our minds cannot conceptualize and our bodies cannot perceive in a tactile way. Social media is a domain where the blueprint is obscured by its architects. How can we contain the fear and anger arising from such placelessness?

Luckily, art materials *are* tactile. Making art is a way to re-engage with the physical world when the opacity and vagueness of social media feel overwhelming. Just as your Big Feelings Box metaphorically contained a challenging feeling, art can be a surrogate for security and trust. You get to define *your* space, control what happens there, and decide what becomes of the process.

Equip Your Space Suit

If the internet is as vast and unknowable as outer space, what type of space suit do you need to explore and thrive?

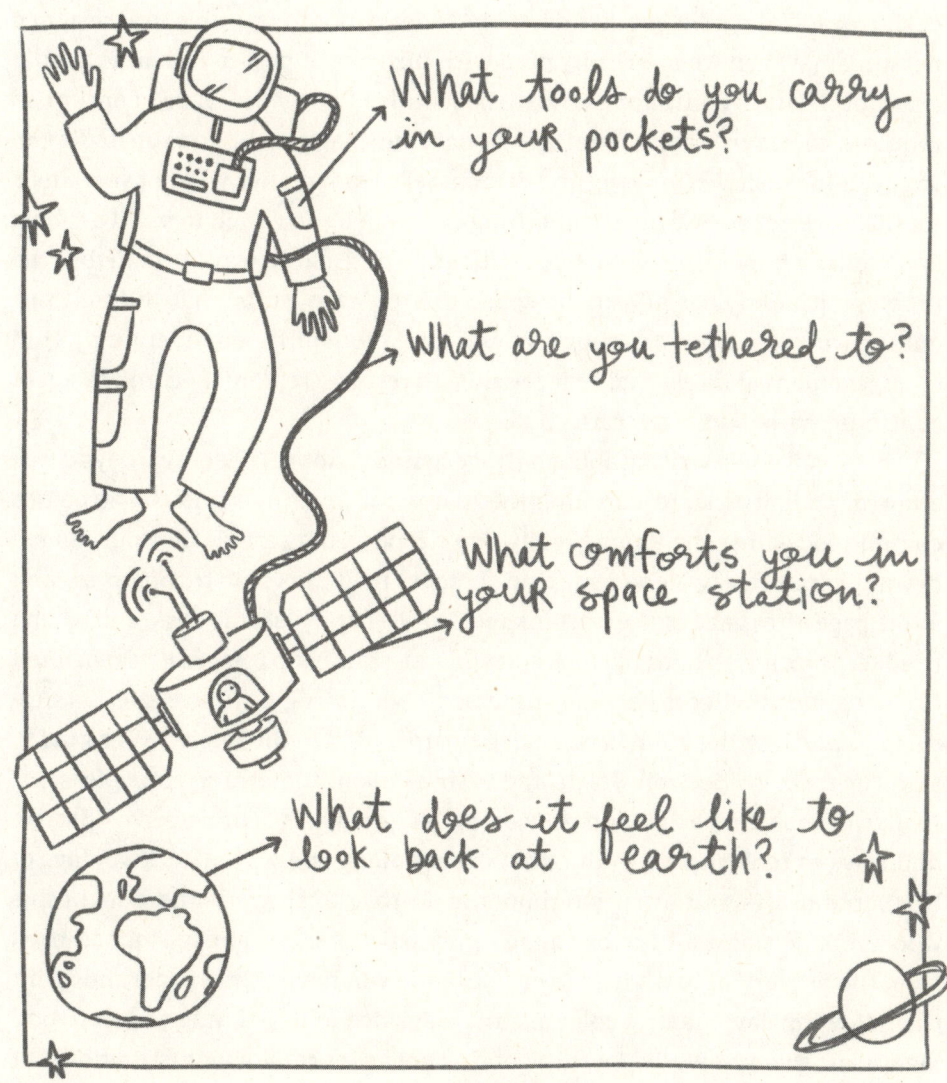

Intermodal Shifts

I don't like the metaphor of a battlefield for describing the task of existing online. There must be another symbol for the struggle to preserve hope in a frontier at war with well-being. Given what we know about the manipulative design of social media, it takes sustained energy not to crumble into resigned pessimism. When we are confronted with misuses of power and bleak predictions for the future, our hope is not to be handled lightly. The type of optimism required to survive the digital age is not one that can be manifested from vague faith. Positive thinking and detachment from reality will not sustain us for the work ahead. We need something concrete upon which to build a robust and realistic hopefulness. We need deliberate *and* gentle ways to confront the problem at hand that affords us space to step away from that toiling to re-engage with the goodness of our lives and relationships. A deliberate rhythm of engagement and rest makes it possible to return—replenished and ready to continue challenging the status quo.

I hit a wall while writing about outrage in this chapter. I spent two days down a horrific rabbit hole, researching the history of Myanmar and the atrocities committed against the Rohingya Muslim people. An internal voice pushed me beyond comfort. I watched graphic footage, read survivor testimonies, and wrote page after page of the unthinkable story. I barely left my desk, and when I tried to sleep, it was hard to stop replaying the traumatic images I'd seen. It felt like my responsibility to become immersed, owing struggle to struggle. I'm sure this was partly white guilt. Who am *I* to turn away from the reality? Who am *I* to stand up from my desk on stolen land to think about something more pleasant?

If we hope to be lifelong advocates for justice, it's imperative that we find ways to tend the wounding that occurs along the way. After two days of belabored drafts and intrusive thoughts, I drove to the city and bought five wooden panels and a tube of Payne's gray paint. I consciously stepped back from the proverbial battlefield (a privilege to even have that choice) and spent the following day pushing color around a surface and listening to Fleetwood Mac. In art therapy, we might think of this not as repression or distraction, but as a creative effort to integrate something we have felt to make room for new insight. An *intermodal shift* is the process of responding to one medium with another. Writing poetry to arrive at the essence of a song. Moving your body to discover how a drawing is living inside you.

Creative response is a proactive way to understand, pause, and process. In the case of this research, stopping to paint was crucial. It helped me interrupt my spinning, digest the information, process the emotions I was feeling, and find the energy to return to it. Burnout occurs when we have no exit from labor and intensity. Though it may be a privilege, it's not selfish to pause when you reach the limits of your capacity. Replenishing your social and emotional capital allows you to sustain care, a crucial ingredient for activism.

Pause + Process

Use this space to intentionally pause. Choose any material you feel called toward, and begin to fill the page. Don't try to plan what you will explore or how it will look. Make a mark. Make another in reply. Keep going until your art tells you it's complete.

Reflect:

How were you feeling before making this? How are you feeling now? Reflect on what shifted when you gave yourself time to stop and create.

_____

_____

_____

_____

_____

_____

_____

_____

_____

Speaking Truth to Power

An asymmetry of power exists on social media. Users cannot see the inner workings of the platforms shaping society and are seldom invited to collaborate on decisions that define the future we will all inherit. But do not confuse disempowerment with powerlessness. Reform can only occur when people bravely speak truth to power. Make your voice heard by using this template to write a letter to a decision-maker about the changes you'd like to see made. You can use this template to write a letter that you actually send or to explore how it might feel to engage in dialogues about societal transformation.

Template:

1. Decide who to write to. Who could you share your opinion with who might have the power to advocate for change?

    Dear _____,

    - the board of your local school district or Parent-Teacher Association
    - the chairpersons of the software-engineering program at a university
    - regulatory bodies for professions that interface with the public (therapists, doctors, social workers, etc.)
    - your city council or municipal government
    - board members of companies and corporations
    - state/provincial/national government representatives with the power to influence legislation

2. Introduce yourself. Share your concerns and explain why this issue is important to you:

    - "I am a parent of two young children. I have watched the impact of social media on my kids' mental health."
    - "I am a social worker. Increasingly, I am seeing my clients impacted by disinformation online."
    - "I am an online business owner. My ability to support my family is dictated by algorithms that I have little control over."
    - "I am a concerned citizen. I am worried about surveillance and persuasive technology design."

3. Describe your hopes for how this person in power will advocate for you and others. *Note: You do not need to be an expert on this topic or offer perfectly crafted solutions! It is the job of people in these positions to advocate for those they represent. You can offer specific ideas or simply ask that they promote your viewpoint in these conversations.*

   › "I would like you to advocate for the creation of an ethical code and regulatory body to oversee the work of software engineers."
   › "I would like to see digital literacy and online safety incorporated into our elementary-school curriculum."
   › "I would like you to be aware of how social media is impacting your constituents' mental health."
   › "I would like you to vote yes/no on Bill #_____."

4. Describe the future you believe is possible:

   › "I believe in supporting children to develop their critical-thinking skills online, so they can care for their mental health in an increasingly digital world."
   › "I believe that social media can be a more equitable space for business owners."
   › "I believe our community can address the impact of racism online."
   › "I believe in a future in which digital platforms prioritize public interest."

5. Thank your local leaders for their advocacy, and gently remind them of their responsibility to represent your concerns:

   › "I appreciate your support for the mental health and well-being of the next generation."
   › "I appreciate your efforts in advocating for the ethical design of social media."
   › "I appreciate your time, and I look forward to witnessing the development of programs that can help increase digital literacy in our region."

   Sincerely,

   [your name]

Write Your Letter:

Dear _____,

I am _____
_____
_____
_____

I would like _____
_____
_____
_____

I believe _____
_____
_____
_____

I appreciate _____
_____
_____
_____

Sincerely,

_____

The Wisdom of Sunflowers

Instead of the metaphor of a battlefield to describe life online, we might think about a sunflower. When radioactive waste poisons a landscape, one strategy for repairing the soil is planting sunflowers. After the Chernobyl and Fukushima nuclear explosions devastated the surrounding environments and communities, fields of sunflowers were sown to begin repairing the contaminated earth. As these plants grow, they pull toxic material out of the soil through a process called phytoremediation. Sunflowers also do a second poetic thing: if you watch one from morning to evening, you'll notice the plant turn to follow the path of the sun traveling through the sky, then staying still after sunset.

We might understand the wisdom of sunflowers like this: it's possible to thrive in hostile landscapes when we transform hurt into beauty, when we stay tethered to our sources of light, when we take time to rest, and when we do it together. The crises of the digital age are not ones we can address with ceaseless effort. This is an era that requires rootedness and rest so that we can sustain momentum over a lifetime.

Take some time to rest by coloring this sunflower.

FEAR + ANGER + DISINFORMATION

HACKS THAT HELP

> I embrace "blocktivism"! No one has the right to be abusive toward me online. Mute, block, and unfollow with wild abandon!

> Part of my activism practice is combating hateful comments online. I keep a folder of prewritten replies so that when I choose to engage, I have language ready. That way, I don't need to spend the emotional energy crafting a perfect comeback.

> I have a rule for myself: I don't DM or comment while angry. I write whatever I want to say on paper and wait twenty-four hours.

> During elections, I take a break from social media. I pick one newspaper to read daily so I'm up to date, but I skip the information overload.

> I try to check in with my deeper intentions before I reply to something critically. Am I educating or advocating? Or am I virtue signaling?

> Choosing where I direct my attention is how I cast my vote for the types of content I want to see thrive online. When I see creators who speak with compassion and nuance, I deliberately interact with their posts. It's a small way of encouraging the culture I want the algorithm to reward.

> Before I engage with something nasty online, I ask myself if it is a good-faith argument. I don't bother fighting with people who are determined to misunderstand me.

HARVEST

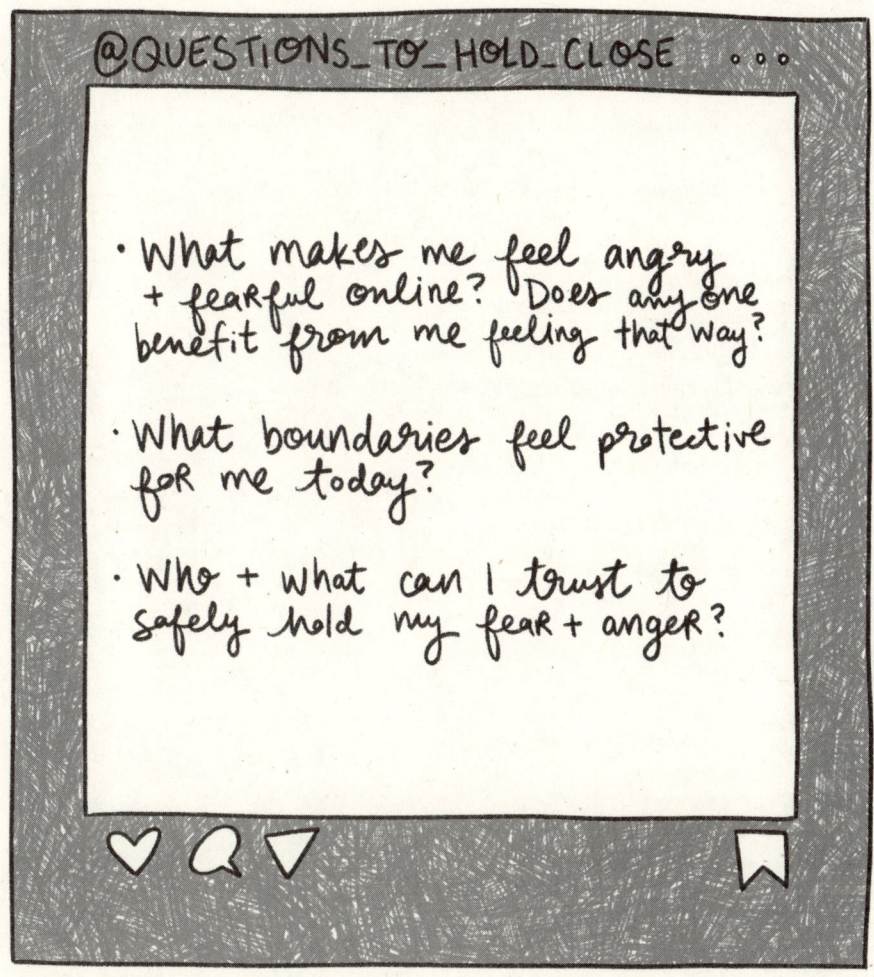

Use these activities to help you distill your reflections about how social media shapes your relationship with productivity. It might be useful to look back at your art and writing as you harvest meaning from this chapter.

Playlist: Songs for Fear + Anger + Disinformation

Take a moment to browse through music you enjoy, and pick:

› A song that calms you down

_____
_____

› A song that feels angry (in a cathartic way!)

_____
_____

› A song with lyrics that are spoken from the heart

_____
_____

Find the Gift

Imagine your exploration of fear, anger, and disinformation has a gift for you. It might be an affirmation, a revelation, or a superpower to take with you into your future digital life. Draw it here.

Quilt Square

Color one side of the square to represent "us" and the other to represent "them." Draw stitches to "sew" the sides together, adding any material or details that makes this feel possible.

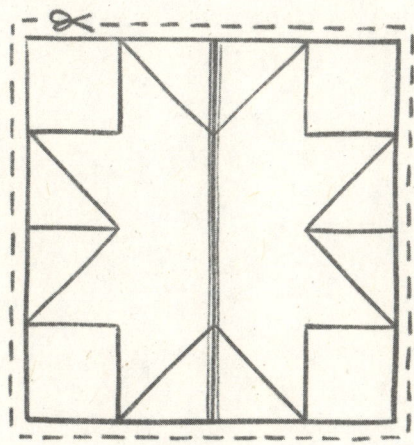

FEAR + ANGER + DISINFORMATION 197

SNIP! SNIP!

CHAPTER 6

PLACE
+
BODY
+
BELONGING

"What is 'real'?" asked the Rabbit one day, when they were lying side by side near the nursery fender, before Nana came to tidy the room. "Does it mean having things that buzz inside you and a stick-out handle?" "Real isn't how you are made," said the Skin Horse. "It's a thing that happens to you. When a child loves you for a long, long time, not just to play with, but *really* loves you, then you become Real."

—*The Velveteen Rabbit* by Margery Williams

In Real Life

I have mixed feelings about the abbreviation IRL ("in real life") to distinguish between the experiences we have online versus offline. We do need a way to describe the palpable difference between these two realms. Each of us knows from our lived experience that a comfortable silence with a dear friend feels different from the simulated eye contact of a video call. Similarly, there is a difference between watching a nature documentary and actually *feeling* the warm grit of a beach as you walk along the coastline.

And yet, I hesitate to draw a line in the proverbial sand and state that our online lives are not "real." This is where we might dive into a debate labyrinth over subjective definitions of what does and doesn't constitute reality. (Sounds philosophical... I'm in!) The quote at the beginning of this chapter comes from a children's book in which a stuffed rabbit is given to a child on Christmas.

The rabbit is quickly forgotten in the excitement of more expensive, mechanical toys. Dejected and yearning for closeness, he asks the Skin Horse, a toy who has lived in the nursery for many years, what it means to be "real." The rabbit is reassured that a sense of reality comes from the care and closeness of relationship.

Defining only the physical realm as reality leaves out the worldviews and spiritual traditions that shape many of our lives. Viewing reality as only observable phenomena also neglects our emotional responses to what happens online and how those experiences impact our mood and behavior offline.

Our emotions are real. Our nervous system's responses to stimuli are real. The care, effort, and thought that go into our digital lives are real too. If my best friend lives an ocean away, and 95 percent of our closeness is mediated by screens, is our connection real? If someone says something nasty about my art online, am I justified in feeling as wounded as if they had said it to my face? As our lives become increasingly steered by the unending corridors of the internet, I feel more unclear about what we mean when we talk about "real life."

Even while appreciating the important and obvious differences between our time online and offline, I'm still not eager to sort my life into clean categories—declaring that offline time is real and good and, therefore, online time is fake and bad.

This is a compassionate caveat to what I will say next. It's important to validate the significance and impact of our digital lives while also holding awareness of the tension between these two domains. When we go to social media to get the bulk of our emotional needs met, we often emerge feeling malnourished—hungry for a variety of connection and groundedness that the internet can't provide. It's an interesting paradox that we could have thousands of online friends and still grapple with pangs of loneliness, or that the infinite landing pages of the internet can leave us feeling unmoored. As human animals, we are wired for tactile, tangible connection. We orient ourselves in physical space and relationship.

I recently moved from a homestead in the middle of nowhere to a small town. That first house was geographically remote; I rarely saw another human being, and there were no friends or businesses within walking distance. My isolation was doubled by the lockdown of the early pandemic, and the internet was the best tool at my disposal for connecting with others. I spent two years in a deep digital immersion without realizing something felt *off*. The discomfort only became clear to me the day after moving into the small town. I took a break from unpacking and walked to the grocery store. I bought a coffee from someone whose name I know and drank it next door with a friend on her patio. I was struck by the sudden and perceptible sense that I was in a *place* again. My body was tingly and energized on the walk back to my new home with a feeling I couldn't quite fit into language. I realized that for two years I'd felt dislocated—craving sustenance that screens hadn't supplied. It was like the feeling of flossing your teeth, dislodging a popcorn kernel from the day before, and noticing relief from a pressure that had gone undetected.

A 2022 study validates what my body was telling me. The research examined the emotional impact of increased use of digital media and communication tools along with decreased time outdoors and fewer face-to-face social interactions during pandemic lockdowns. The results showed a correlation between these factors and feelings of depersonalization. *Depersonalization* and *derealization* refer to a clinical description of feeling estranged from yourself, your body, and the world around you. The study also showed that those who reported higher feelings of depersonalization, resulting from lockdown isolation and a hyper-digitized lifestyle, also experienced negative emotions more vividly.[1] Time online has a legitimate impact on our sense of self, connection, and well-being.

We need belonging and groundedness to thrive—including an intimacy with people, nature, and our own bodies. When we spend a great deal of our lives online, we might unknowingly be grasping for something the digital world is not equipped to provide. It's as if we are panning for gold in a chlorine swimming pool. Deliberately cultivating a sense of place and community beyond our screens is crucial to our well-being. This doesn't mean social media is not a useful or meaningful tool. A swimming pool might be a perfect place for leisure or exercise, but it's also an environment deliberately controlled by tile, filters, and lifeguards to serve a specific purpose. If we try to mine for something precious there, we may emerge soaked and wondering if we're incapable of obtaining it or, worse, that it doesn't exist at all.

This chapter is about coming home to ourselves, the people around us, and the land we live on.

The Philosopher's Encyclopedia

Imagine you are a professor of your own philosophy of life. Which feelings and experiences are personal examples of what feels "real"? You don't need to justify or explain why these things hold a texture of reality or depth for you. Write down the first examples that come to mind.

What feels truly real for me is _____

What feels truly real for me is _____

What feels truly real for me is _____

What feels truly real for me is _____

What feels truly real for me is _____

What feels truly real for me is _____

What feels truly real for me is _____

What feels truly real for me is _____

What feels truly real for me is _____

What feels truly real for me is _____

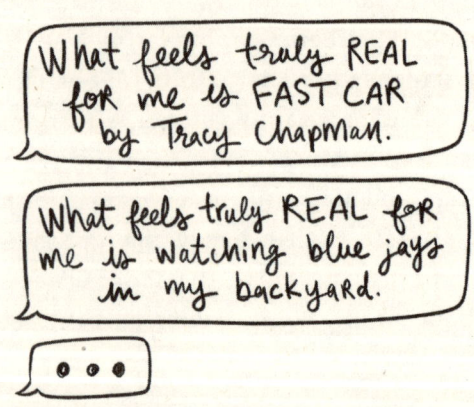

The Dangers of Fake Community

I am guilty of using the word *community* loosely. In my job, I use that word to describe digital gathering spaces where people log on to video calls, create art, chat, and pay me to facilitate. It is communal, in the sense that we are together, making and sharing. On message boards, people post pictures of their art and say nice things to one another. I invite other art therapists to host the group and collaborate with participants to choose themes to explore in future weeks.

Writer and feminist marketing consultant Kelly Diels warns of the dangers of "fake" communities we find online, offering that we often romanticize the connections formed in online groups, drawing on the language of "community" to describe a sense of safety and mutual care that doesn't always exist there. Diels defines *true* community as a space where power is held laterally, not by a single person. There are elders and peers with diverse perspectives. *Real communities* foster horizontal relationships, where members show up to support one another outside of the specific goals or interests that initially formed the group. Communities are also usually bound by in-person connections and places. Because of the physical experience, members feel accountable to resolve conflict and collaborate on shaping the culture of the group.[2] When we speak about community, are we talking about a circle that nurtures mutual support, power, collaboration, and responsibility? Or are we borrowing the language of an intimacy we crave?

This is not to say a Facebook group for new parents or a book club hosted by an author can't provide a type of belonging. Having *all* your needs for community met in person is a privilege that many don't have consistent access to. It might be true that you feel your most free, authentic, and cared for online. If you are a trans teenager in a state that is trying to criminalize your existence, a message board with others like you might be a true source of care. If you are the only person in your friend group living with chronic illness, social media groups may be valuable spaces to commiserate and seek advice. Despite this potential for connection, if you have a full schedule of online meetups and it still feels like something is lacking, it's not because you're not doing enough. You might simply be craving the types of connection that aren't found in controlled digital environments.

This is because *mutual regulation* or *co-regulation* happens in relationship. Our autonomic nervous systems take cues from the autonomic nervous systems of the people around us. If you've ever felt yourself soothed by a hug or the active listening of a calm parent or partner, then you've experienced this. If another person's presence seems to put you at ease, it's because our bodies pick up on nonverbal cues from other people's bodies. Close relationships and trust are forged when we receive feedback that we are safe in someone's company. This phenomenon is most obvious when we share physical proximity. Although it may be possible to feel that reassuring attunement with someone during a video call, we can't quite find it in a comment section or an email. A genuine sense of belonging and connection comes from more than words alone. It comes from the way our bodies communicate with each other.

The Limits of Digital Community

Take a moment to reflect on the online communities you belong to. This could be something structured like a membership or message board. This could also be a looser association, like a hashtag you use or a general topic you engage with on social media. What do you gain from this gathering space? Which of your needs are met there? Which of your needs are not met there?

Examples:
› A community I belong to online is: *A Facebook group of people who graduated from the same school as me.*
› What feels nourishing about participating in this community is: *Alumni offer career advice and understand the unique challenges of our field.*
› This community doesn't offer me enough: *One-on-one connection, time to make art together in silence, the sound of each other laughing.*

A community I belong to online is:

What feels nourishing about participating in this community is:

This community doesn't offer me enough:

A community I belong to online is:

What feels nourishing about participating in this community is:

_____
_____

This community doesn't offer me enough:

_____
_____

A community I belong to online is:

_____
_____

What feels nourishing about participating in this community is:

_____
_____

This community doesn't offer me enough:

_____
_____

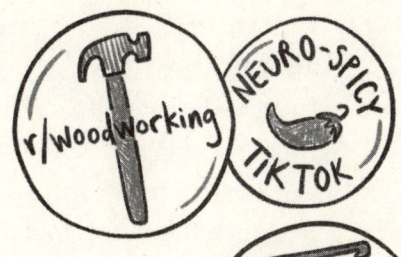

Club Swag

Pick the online community that is the most meaningful to you. Create a button that you could imagine wearing proudly on your clothes to signify your belonging.

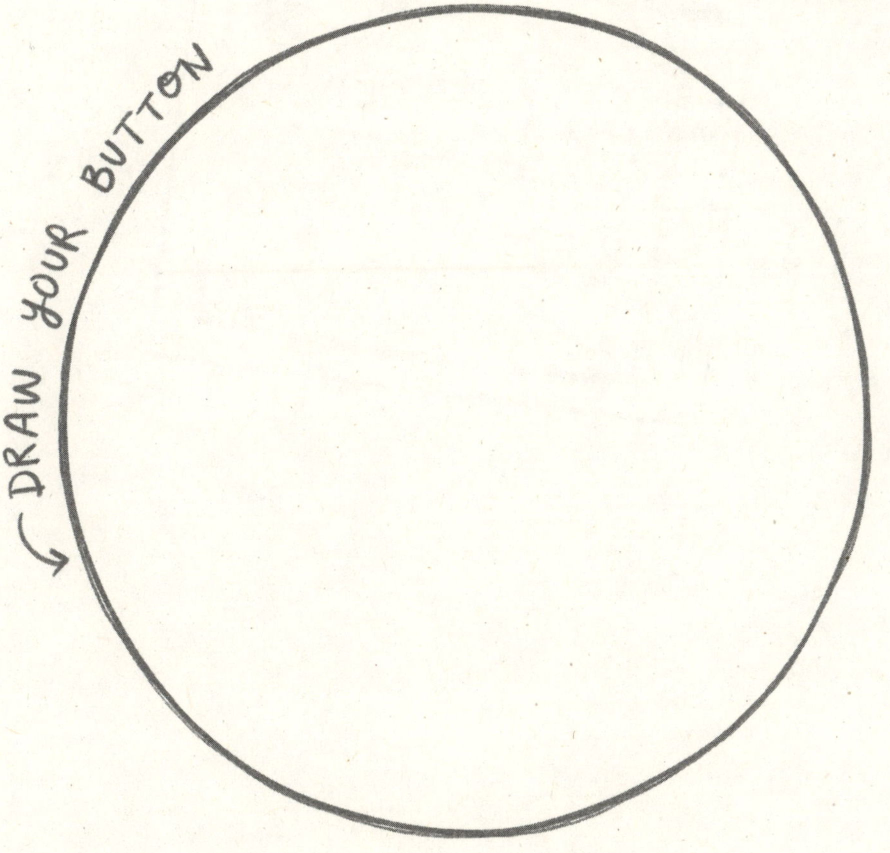

← DRAW YOUR BUTTON

Address Zine

Do you want to tend to the relationships that make up your in-person community? Gather the home addresses and phone numbers of the people who are most important to you and write them in this zine (a mini, handmade magazine). Cut it out, fold it, and staple it together. Next time you're craving connection, use your address book to reach out by phone or snail mail.

BACK COVER | FRONT COVER

NAME:
PHONE:
ADDRESS:

WHAT'S
IMPORTANT
TO THEM:

NAME:
PHONE:
ADDRESS:

WHAT'S
IMPORTANT
TO THEM:

NAME:
PHONE:
ADDRESS:

WHAT'S
IMPORTANT
TO THEM:

NAME:
PHONE:
ADDRESS:

WHAT'S
IMPORTANT
TO THEM:

FOLD

PLACE + BODY + BELONGING

↙ FOLD

✂ -

NAME: _____	NAME: _____
PHONE: _____	PHONE: _____
ADDRESS: _____	ADDRESS: _____
_____	_____
WHAT'S _____	WHAT'S _____
IMPORTANT _____	IMPORTANT _____
TO THEM: _____	TO THEM: _____
_____	_____

NAME: _____	NAME: _____
PHONE: _____	PHONE: _____
ADDRESS: _____	ADDRESS: _____
_____	_____
WHAT'S _____	WHAT'S _____
IMPORTANT _____	IMPORTANT _____
TO THEM: _____	TO THEM: _____
_____	_____

NAME: _____	NAME: _____
PHONE: _____	PHONE: _____
ADDRESS: _____	ADDRESS: _____
_____	_____
WHAT'S _____	WHAT'S _____
IMPORTANT _____	IMPORTANT _____
TO THEM: _____	TO THEM: _____
_____	_____

Snail Mail

Pick someone from your address book and use this envelope to send them an analog "hello." Draw a picture of a memory or an inside joke you share with this person.

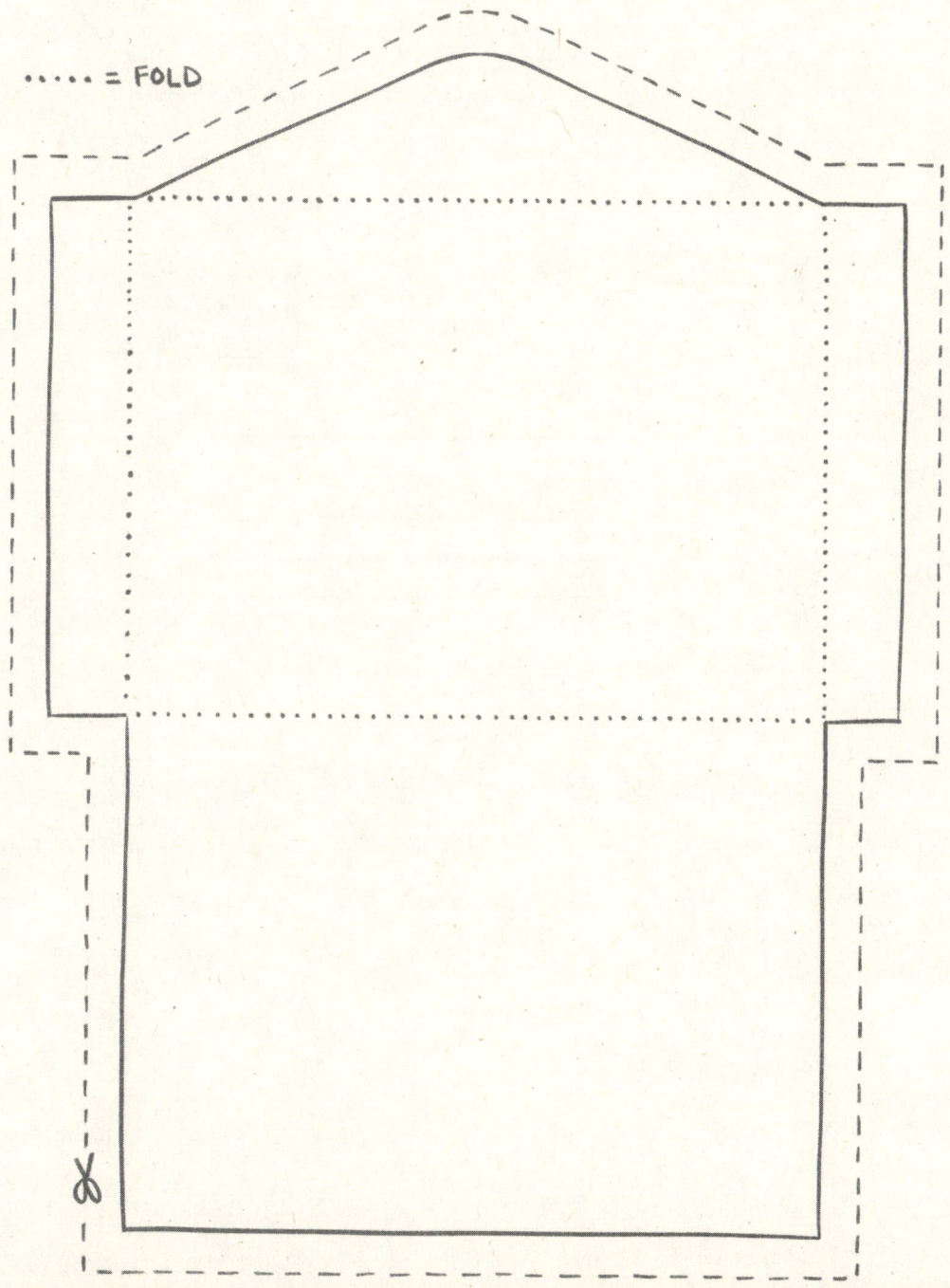

Fill in your address and theirs.

Once you're done, cut out your envelope. Fold the sides toward the center and secure them with tape. Now you're ready to add a stamp and send your card in the mail!

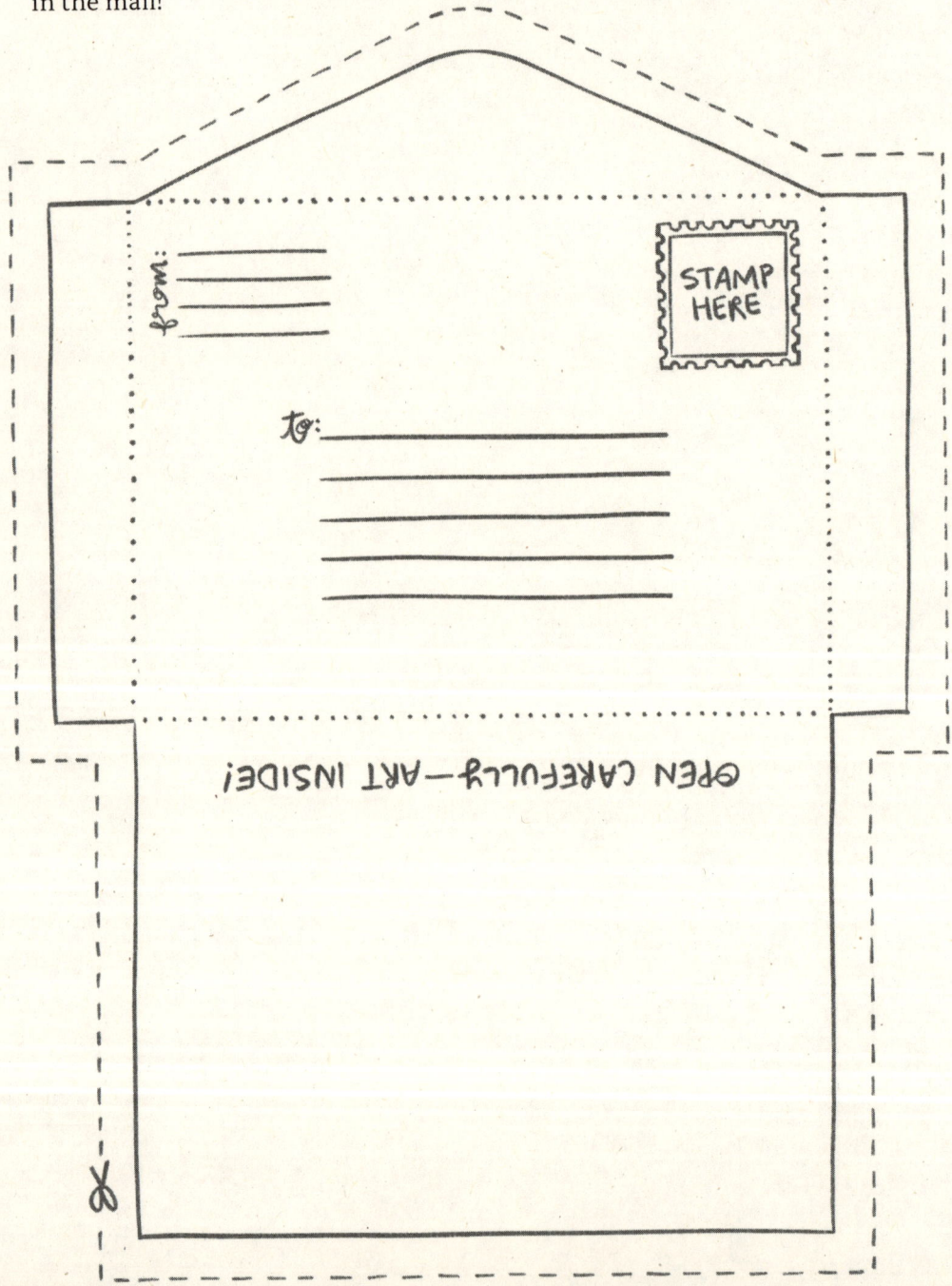

Neighborhood Poem

If you want to feel a deeper sense of community with the people around you, where can you start? It can feel daunting to begin the task of cultivating community, especially if you're at a stage of life without built-in social circles like a school or office. Familiarity takes time, and patience for this type of intimacy can be painful when we yearn to belong. Common advice, such as "Go meet people at your local coffee shop!" or "Join a club or sports league!" may not feel possible if you experience anxiety in new social situations.

Use this template to write a poem with your neighbors. Start by writing the first line of a poem. Then cut out this poster and put it somewhere in public for your neighbors to find. You could tape it to a phone pole or pin it to the bulletin board at a local business. Leave a pen attached to a string so others can add their own lines to the poem. Go back in a few days to see what you have created in collaboration with your community!

NEIGHBORHOOD POEM

Let's write a poem together! Read the words above + add a line of your own.

THANKS NEIGHBOR!

— SNIP! SNIP! —

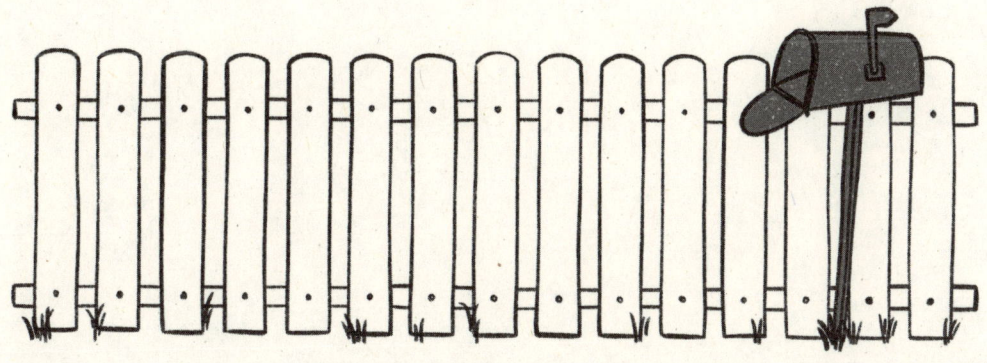

Community Comic

Now try telling a story with your neighbors! Start this comic strip with a quick drawing and an opening line describing how the story begins. Leave it in a different public place with a pen so others can add to it. Check back in a few days to see what you have created in collaboration with your community.

SNIP! SNIP!

Reflect:

› What happened when you created something with your neighbors?
    _____
    _____
    _____

› What did it feel like to check back on the poem or comic strip?
    _____
    _____
    _____

› What was interesting or surprising about the art that emerged?
    _____
    _____
    _____

Take a Mayor Walk

This idea comes from my brilliant internet friend, Anna Seirian. Anna is a neurodivergent creative and cofounder of Spacetime Monotasking, a company that designs productivity tools for distracted people. She came up with the Mayor Walk as a practice for feeling connected to the people she encounters in her community.

How it works:

Take yourself on a walk around your neighborhood while pretending to be the local mayor. This means greeting each person you pass with a "Hi, there!" and a smile, or maybe a "Gosh, this is nice weather we're having!" Your goal isn't to have long or deep conversations. The people you greet don't even need to respond. Cosplaying as a host or ambassador can make it easier to experiment with being more extroverted than usual. Anna adds, "When you're the mayor, everyone is excited to see you, so it helps you embody that your presence is valuable without doing much, and that small acts of friendliness could make a stranger's day."[3]

How might you move through your neighborhood differently if you pretended it was your job to foster warm connections?

This Is Your Body on Social Media

Lost in a blur of apps and notifications, have you ever been suddenly rattled back into the here and now?

Your fridge has been left open, and the door begins beeping.

You feel a sharp ache in your back. You've been sitting in discomfort for minutes without realizing it.

You smell something burning on the stove.

Your partner speaks louder, now annoyed: "Did you hear what I just said?"

You drop your phone on your face while lying in bed.

Most of us have had the experience of being jolted back into reality from the fog of social media. It's a commonplace experience that points to the ways our phones can override the sensations in our bodies. If *flow* is a state of fluidity between the mind and body while being deeply engaged in a task (think: painting or running), then scrolling might be its opposite: all immersion, with little awareness of what is occurring in your body beyond the perimeter of your screen.

Why is it so hard to listen to our bodies when we are engaged with our phones? One explanation is that our bodies are programmed to survive by seeking satisfaction. By design, social media is *too* good at giving the body what it craves. *Neuroadaption*, or the tolerance we build after repeated exposure to a reward, explains why it can feel harder to find pleasure in other activities when we consistently engage with high-dopamine experiences. Over time we need more engagement to feel the same degree of satisfaction that the behavior initially offered us.[4] One way I've noticed this in my own life is when I repeatedly check the same apps over and over, unconsciously hoping for a new notification or more stimulating content—hence, the design of a newsfeed that can be endlessly refreshed. Social media's open faucet of dopamine makes it more challenging to enjoy (or tolerate) activities that provide smaller doses of pleasure.

I once complained to my therapist about how tough it felt to put down my phone. She asked earnestly, "So, what feels better than scrolling?" I paused to really think about it. The first words to cross my mind were *Honestly, not much.*

But I didn't admit that to her. I felt ashamed, like maybe I'd broken my brain or had become a deeply uninteresting person. It's not that I don't derive pleasure from other things; it's just that the pull toward my phone often feels so much stronger than my motivation to go outside or start a new painting.

As a person with ADHD, task initiation is one facet of executive functioning I struggle with. Because my brain processes dopamine differently than a neurotypical person, summoning the effort to do something that's good for me often feels like an insurmountable task. As a result, behaviors that offer an immediate reward are incredibly hard to resist. Grabbing a granola bar is more accessible than combining five ingredients in a blender. Watching a reality show is more accessible than reading the subtitles of a documentary in a foreign language.

The problem, for both neurodivergent and neurotypical folks, is that with repeated exposure, the brain becomes so accustomed to the immediate gratification of social media that it's harder to do the slow work of seeking pleasure elsewhere. Even though I *know* that moving my body will ultimately feel better than doomscrolling, on a low-capacity day, the habit of opening Instagram feels more doable than standing, lacing up my shoes, and going outside for a walk. It's even harder to take the scenic route to well-being when I've spent months or years carving out the neural pathway of seeking relief, habitually, though screen time.

Our minds and bodies are interconnected. Luckily, our bodies are portals back to presence and into a sense of being real. In his book *My Grandmother's Hands: Racialized Trauma and the Pathways to Mending Our Hearts and Bodies*, psychotherapist and anti-racism educator Resmaa Menakem explores why our bodies are central to both personal and collective healing. He writes, "The body, not the thinking brain, is where we experience most of our pain, pleasure, and joy, and where we process most of what happens to us. It is also where we do most of our healing, including our emotional and psychological healing. And it is where we experience resilience and a sense of flow."[5]

Intentionally engaging with the physical experience of ourselves and the world is a protective and reparative practice in the digital age. Think of your body not as a chore or a dependent, but as an ally in wellness.

art therapist tip:

When Embodiment Isn't Easy

Conversations about embodiment need to be sensitive to the many reasons we might feel unsafe or unable to connect with the physical experience of our bodies.

If we have experienced trauma, then moving quickly toward the site of that memory or violation can be triggering. Our bodies may also be the subject of shame due to the pervasive cultural indoctrination that certain skin colors, ages, abilities, sizes, and genders are more worthy than others. Receiving the persistent message that our bodies are not worthy of care, belonging, or safety is a type of chronic trauma. Witnessing the oppression of people who look like us is also a type of chronic trauma.

When we are met with danger, our bodies are naturally skilled at protecting us. Sometimes the body decides it is safer to dissociate (disconnect from itself and its surroundings) than endure the unbearable. Trauma healing involves the slow and very gentle process of returning to the body and learning to trust that we are safe inside it.

If being with your body isn't easy today, go slowly, return later, or skip these exercises entirely. Listening to your internal sense of what feels safe is more valuable than any of these activities. (Perhaps skipping an activity *is* a way of being in solidarity with your body!) If embodiment is a topic that feels challenging, it may be helpful to work with a somatic therapist or other trauma-informed health professional.

Dropping into Sensation

Reflect on both the comfortable and uncomfortable sensations your body experiences when you spend time online.

What happens in your body right before you pick up your phone?

_____
_____
_____

What sensations do you notice while you're scrolling? What sensations *don't* you notice?

_____
_____
_____

How does your body tell you that you've spent more time online than is comfortable?

_____
_____
_____

How do you feel physically after you've spent time staring at a screen? How long does that sensation last? What shifts it?

_____
_____
_____

Some of these sensations might be subtle! Social media is so engrossing that you might not notice how it feels in your body to scroll or when you begin to tip toward discomfort. If these questions feel tough to answer, try this:

› Set a timer for five minutes to intentionally scroll.
› Notice what happens in the moment before you pick up your phone. Scan your body for any shifts in emotion or sensation. What does the anticipation actually feel like? Does it have a location, tightness, rhythm, or other presence?
› Open an app more slowly than usual. Does the anticipation change? Does anything in your body change?
› When your timer goes off, tune in to your body again. What can you physically feel now? Try to name a few sensations you notice.
› Continue to scroll while holding a gentle awareness of the sensations you experience. Look for physical cues that it's time to sign off. How does your body tell you it's ready to do something different?

Hand Tracing

Practice hanging out with your body by tracing your hands. Lay your hand against this page and pause for a moment to press each fingertip into the paper. Feel your skin make contact and notice the texture of the page. If your hand goes over the edges of the workbook, notice how the sensations are different for the parts of your hand that extend beyond the paper. Now slowly trace the shape of your hand. Pay attention to the feeling of the pencil moving around the curve of each finger and see if you can follow the sensation all the way around as you create an outline. (Note: It's okay to draw over the words and illustrations!)

Try it again with your opposite hand. Does this hand experience pressure and texture in a similar or different way? What does it feel like to hold a pen and trace the outline with your nondominant hand?

Ask your hands about their favorite and least favorite sensations. Inside the outlines, draw and write about the things they love to engage with. On the outside of the outline, draw and write about the sensations they dislike.

I love moss, fidget spinners, + gloves!

I hate chalk, steel wool, + sunscreen.

Sensory Ritual for Connecting with Your Body

Go back to your sensory scavenger hunt from chapter 1. Choose a favorite sensation to become the cue for a ritual of connecting with yourself. This could be a specific smell, taste, sound, feeling, or visual symbol you use as a reminder to put down your phone and be with your body.

Examples:

- When I **smell lavender essential oil**, I want to remind myself that **it's safe to be in my home and my body** so that I can **get ready to have a restful sleep**.
- When I **put on my fuzzy slippers in the morning**, I want to remind myself that **there is no urgency to respond to emails first thing** so that I can **relax while I drink my coffee**.

Fill in the blanks:

When I **(sensory cue)**, I want to remind myself that **(a kind message)** so that I can **(experience you'd like to associate with this sensation)**.

When I _____,

I want to remind myself that _____

_____

so that I can _____

_____

Bonus Craft!

Is there something you can do to elevate the object you use in your ritual? Design a new label for your favorite essential oil! Place your headphones on a cute tray! Embroider a message on the sleeve of your bathrobe!

art therapist tip:

Peeing: An Act of Solidarity

Do you have to pee?
Go right now.
Don't wait until after you've finished this page.
Go right now.

Welcome back!

If you're in the habit of ignoring your body's signals for attention, using the bathroom as soon as you notice you need to is a place to start. Not at the end of the video you're watching. Not when the email you're drafting is done. Not after all the dishes are clean and put away. You don't need to wait until you've been "productive enough." You deserve relief and comfort exactly as you are. It's an act of solidarity with your body to respond to its requests with timely care.

If this were a conversation with your bladder, pausing from responsibilities or distraction to pee would be like saying to your body, *I hear you. Your safety and comfort is important to me, and you can trust me to give you what you need.*

Take it a step further: Spend longer than necessary washing your hands. Be picky finding the water temperature that feels the best on your skin. Linger in the warmth. You're worth the patience it takes for a small moment of pleasure.

Before you continue reading:

Is there anything else your body wants or needs right now? Lip balm? Stretchier pants? To call in sick from work? Take an extra moment to do something that makes you physically comfortable.

Walking as Art Practice

The sales associate was patient and a little pitying when I tried to pronounce "compass" in Czech. Eventually I showed him Google Translate on my screen. He nodded with a click of recognition, led me to a stack of small boxes, and handed me a black plastic circle that fit in the palm of my hand.

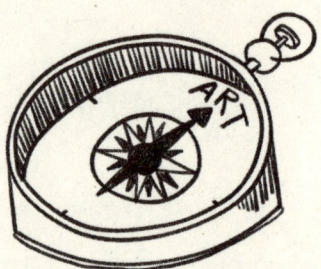

I was twenty-three, spending the month in Prague while training to be an English teacher, and beginning to feel unglued. My life fit into a backpack, and the rigorous program didn't leave much space to get my bearings in a new city. I had chosen this adventure, but I hadn't expected to feel so dislocated. I was missing a sense of connection to my home, my body, and my art. Feeling uprooted in the first days of living in an unfamiliar place and overwhelmed by my workload, I thought of Richard Long and Marina Abramović. They are both artists who walk *as art*. Long would repeat the same path through tall grass until his steps parted a trail: a trace of his body in nature. Abramović and her life/performance partner, Ulay, walked from opposite ends of the Great Wall of China. Their meeting in the middle became the ceremonial end to their twelve-year relationship. I thought about how these artists walked as a way of cultivating presence with their surroundings. Long and Abramović embarked on pilgrimages toward place—and also toward self.

I decided the solution to my dis-ease was to walk every morning for the period of a month and photograph the compass in the places I found myself.

The ritual was simple: wake up early, pull the compass over my neck (more as a symbol than a tool), and wander. Sometimes I'd deliberately get lost, only pulling out my phone for directions home as a last resort. Sometimes I'd find crumbling buildings, forests in the middle of the city, or a really good bakery. Everything feels like a discovery when you haven't decided what you're looking for. This practice continued when I moved to Hanoi, where I got lost almost every day, exploring twisty alleyways that spit me out in unexpected places. Walking became my remedy for feeling adrift. Comforting myself with the familiarity of that ritual helped me navigate the transition and turbulence of my early twenties.

But walking isn't just useful when arriving in a new place. If I'm being honest, I've often felt this same dislocation at home. Perhaps it's the seclusion of rural living or the legacy of early-pandemic isolation combined with being a chronically online human. Sometimes my center of gravity feels like it exists in digital space rather than on the physical land I live on. The internet's vastness and busyness can feel like being dropped into the center of an unfamiliar city.

Practices that ground us in the physical experience of place can help us arrive over and over again in our own bodies and neighborhoods. I think of walking as a way of nurturing intimacy with our environment. It offers us *placefulness*. This is a word I like to use for experiencing our surroundings in a tactile way—being conscious of *being somewhere*. Placefulness exists in stark contrast to the place*less*ness of the internet, where we are seemingly everywhere and nowhere simultaneously.

When we walk the same route repeatedly—the path to the bus stop, the corner store, the dog park—we can practice a ritual of intimacy with our surroundings, paying attention to the nuance of "real life." As the poet David Whyte wrote, "Alertness is the hidden discipline of familiarity."[6] Wandering our neighborhoods can become a sort of apprenticeship with the mundane that reminds us of the landscape, people, and histories that hold us.

Neighborhood Map

Draw a map from memory of the place you currently live. No need for accuracy! Include places that are familiar or important to you. Include symbols for different relationships or memories that have occurred here.

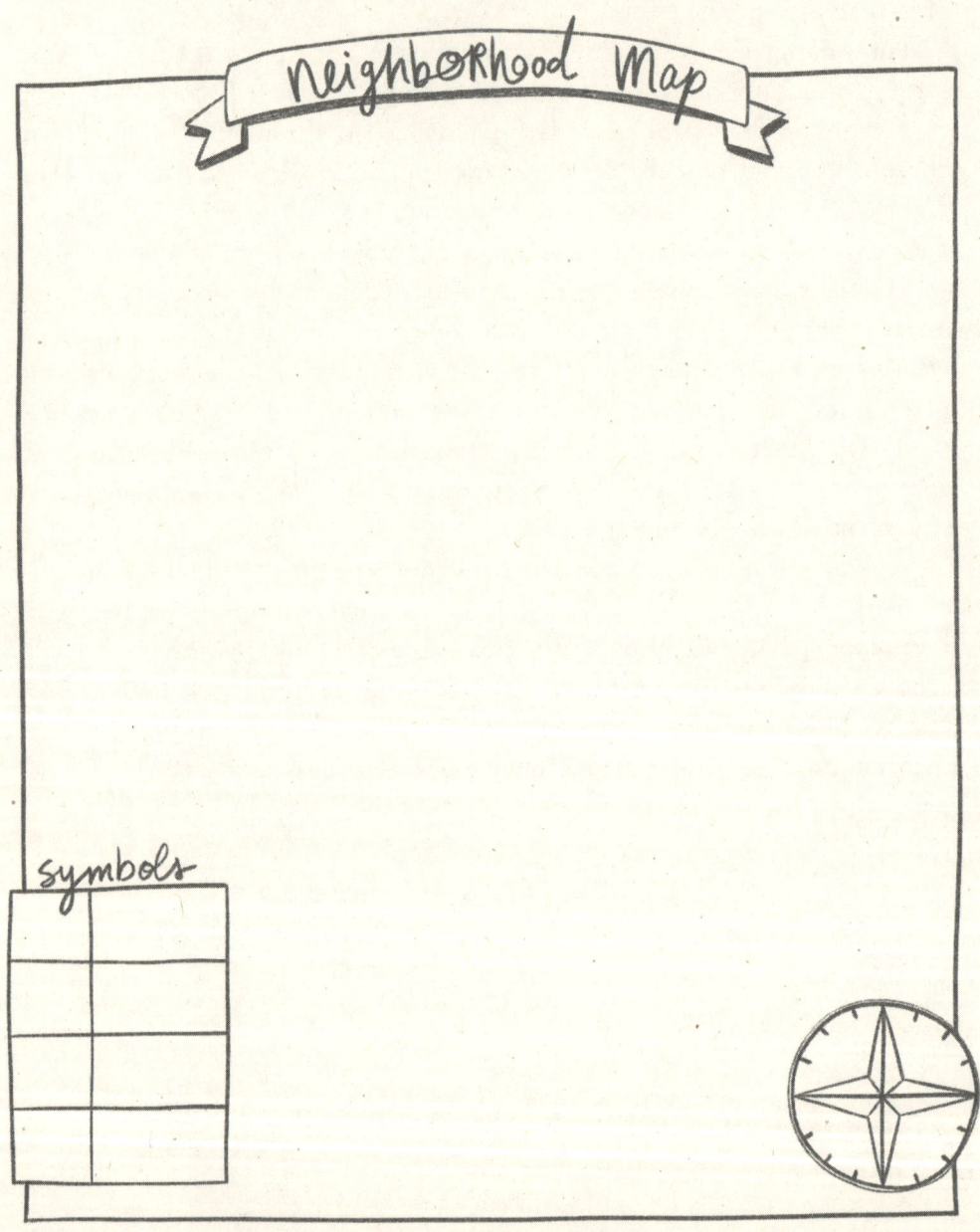

Search History Map

If your search history or most frequently used apps were a neighborhood, what would the map look like? Draw it below, adding symbols to the key for sites of interest, relationships, or emotions.

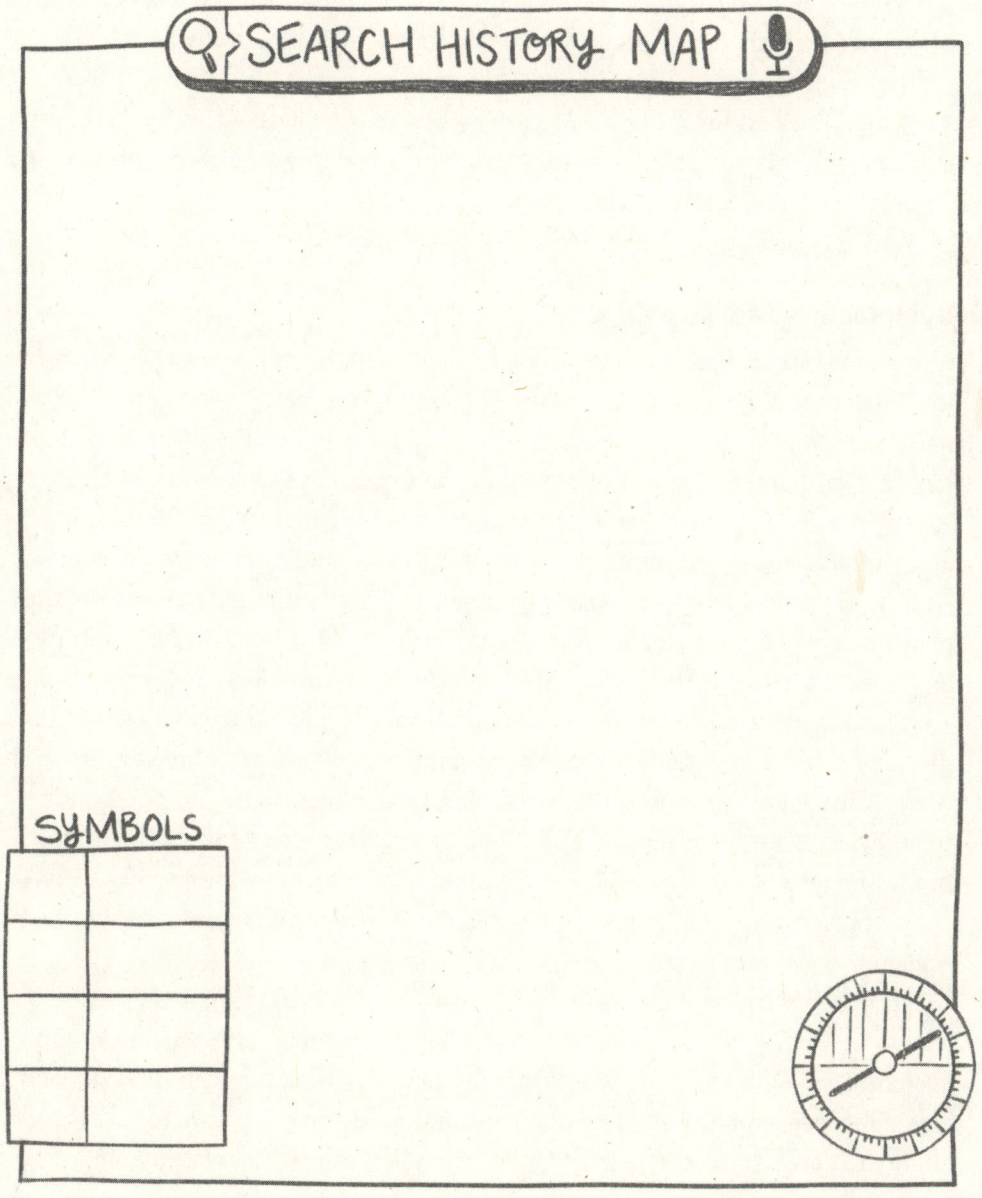

The Stories Places Tell

Human beings tell stories to make sense of life and imbue our world with meaning. If you're curious about the place you live, use these prompts to begin researching your surroundings.

› Who lived in your house before you? What was important to them?
› What is the history of your city or neighborhood? What drew people to this location? Who thrived here? Who didn't?
› Which Indigenous group lived here before settlers arrived? What is their name for this place? What is their creation story (mythology about the origin of the world)?
› Which plants and animals are native to this land?

Symbiosis + Stewardship

Cultivating intimacy with place is urgently needed in the face of our climate crisis. We know that connecting with nature is good for our mental health, but seeing nature as a space that exists solely in service of *our* well-being is the attitude that has enabled humanity to colonize, pollute, and extract the earth to the brink of apocalypse. Environmental activist and author Joanna Macy states, "We have acted as if we could know and control the world from the outside, as if we were separate from it. We came to think of ourselves as made of better stuff than the animals and plants and rocks and water around us. And our technologies of the last centuries amplified disastrously the ecological effects of that assumption."[7]

A feeling of numbness or disconnection from the natural world makes sense given how much of our lives are lived in digital non-places. Numbness is also an understandable response to the increasing frequency of climate panic in the news cycle. If we had the time and capacity to grieve every forest fire, oil spill, hurricane, or extinct species, we might feel frozen by rage and sorrow. I don't think the answer is staying parked in despair. Action requires momentum and responsiveness, not paralysis.

When we reframe our role in nature from one of extraction to stewardship, we acknowledge our interconnectedness—and responsibility—within a living system. The goodness that comes from an intimacy with place goes far beyond a personal sense of groundedness. It is *from* that intimacy that we feel a responsibility to care for the earth. Everyone thrives in a symbiotic relationship.

Notes from the Field

Take yourself outside to connect with nature, and bring your workbook with you. Study the things around you. Instead of looking up the names of plants, animals, or minerals on your phone, make a quick drawing and note the features you observe. Imagine you are in conversation with the land and creatures and that they speak back to you.

Something that...

IS A COLOR I LOVE:

What I like about it:

What it likes about me:

MOVES IN AN INTERESTING WAY:

What I like about it:

What it likes about me:

HAS A UNIQUE TEXTURE:

What I like about it:

What it likes about me:

HAS A DISTINCT SMELL:

What I like about it:

What it likes about me:

I'VE NEVER NOTICED BEFORE:

What I like about it:

What it likes about me:

I'VE SEEN A MILLION TIMES:

What I like about it:

What it likes about me:

Bring the Outdoors Online

Pick the ten people from your contacts that you communicate with most often. Go for a walk outside with your phone and snap a picture of a plant, animal, or mineral that reminds you of each person. Change each person's contact photo to the natural element that feels like a metaphor for their personality. Now, every time they call or text, you'll be reminded of how your relationship is mirrored by nature. Inversely, every time you see that plant, animal, or mineral, you'll think of the associated person.

Becoming Real

The Velveteen Rabbit story could be a metaphor for the layered realities we interface with as both citizens of digital space and stewards of the physical world. In the beginning of the story, the Skin Horse consoles the rabbit, assuring him that "real" is something we become when we feel connected to others. Over time, the child chooses the rabbit, and it is through their closeness that the rabbit first feels secure within himself.

This sense of realness is soothing, until the rabbit is left outside and meets *actual* rabbits: the kind who can hop on their hind legs and aren't sewn together from fabric. He longs to also experience *that* degree of embodied realness. When the child falls ill with scarlet fever, the doctor orders that all his toys be burned. In his grief and yearning, a spell is cast on the rabbit. A fairy turns him into a wild rabbit so that he can join the others. He is elated at the discovery of his body, his ability to dance in the forest, and his new life in the company of others like him. The story ends when the rabbit returns to the garden to visit the child, who "never knew that it really was his own Bunny, come back to look at the child who had first helped him to be Real."[8]

The Velveteen Rabbit is real twice: first, in the closeness of love with the child; and then eternally, when he arrives in his body, goes outside, and begins a life among living, breathing animals.

We don't need to discount the limited "realness" we find online. The love between the child and the rabbit was a stepping stone. It was profound and meaningful, despite being abridged by circumstances outside their control. The enduring realness, however, came from being welcomed into the world outside of the nursery.

Inhabiting our bodies, grounding in place and nature, and tending to reciprocal relationships is how we protect the stunning and fragile realness of being human in the digital age.

HACKS THAT HELP

> I stand up when I check my phone. Moving into an active position helps me remember how my body feels and keeps me from getting lost in scrolling for as long as I'm sitting.

> I don't bring my phone on dog walks. I want to be present when I'm moving outdoors.

> Technology helps me be a better friend! I set reminders in my phone calendar to reach out to the people I care about, and I keep a spreadsheet of gift ideas, important dates, and other details to remember.

> When I have a question, I try to pause before searching for the answer online so I can savor the wondering. This also keeps me from accidentally ending up distracted on another app.

> When I get together with friends, we put our phones in a box so we don't automatically reach for social media when there's a lull in conversation.

> I disable all notifications except for texts and phone calls. I don't want to be interrupted when I'm in nature or with people I care about.

HARVEST

@QUESTIONS_TO_HOLD_CLOSE

- What do my online communities offer me? What don't they offer me?

- How does my body respond to time on social media? How does it communicate its needs to me?

- How do I foster connection with the people + places that exist beyond my screen?

Use these activities to help you distill your reflections about how social media shapes your attention. It might be useful to look back at your art and writing as you harvest meaning from this chapter.

PLACE + BODY + BELONGING

Playlist: Songs for Place + Body + Belonging

Take a moment to browse through music you enjoy, and pick:

› A song that feels like the landscape you live in

　_____

　_____

› A song your body wants to move to

　_____

　_____

› A song that reminds you of a person you love

　_____

　_____

Find the Gift

Imagine your exploration of place, body, and belonging has a gift for you. It might be an affirmation, a revelation, or a superpower to take with you into your future digital life. Draw it here.

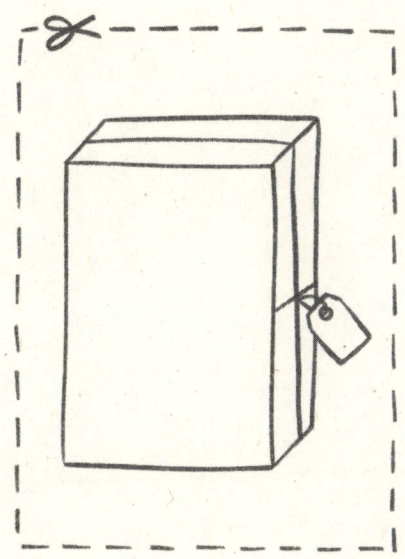

Quilt Square

Choose a color or pattern to represent your body, your community, and the land you live on. Fill in the spaces of this quilt square in any order or arrangement that feels right. "Sew" the panels together with stitches drawn in a color that represents the bond between them.

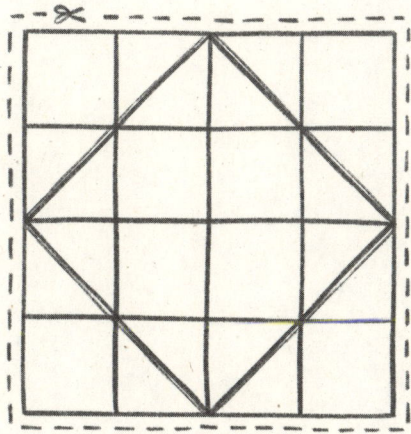

- SNIP! SNIP! -

CHAPTER 7

STITCHING IT ALL TOGETHER

Soft Work

We began our time together on these pages with the metaphor of quilt-making. Just like a quilt, the soft work of thriving online occurs in layers. Some things may feel clear: pieced together and matching at the corners. Other parts of your investigation may remain invisible: obscured between layers of fabric, known only by touch and attention, and not visible on the surface.

Here's the thing about quilts: They are made cohesive by a joining of parts. Even when the fabric doesn't align in crisp edges and the thread tangles itself *again*, you can still gather the pieces into a whole. What I've learned is that you can make a quilt from scraps of clothing and use an old fleece blanket as batting. Crooked and meandering stitches will hold your effort together as well as precise, parallel seams. You can create an object of comfort, warmth, and legacy from what you already have.

I've learned that the closing ceremony of making a quilt is binding the edges and closing the frayed sides with a border that wraps around the story. This is not an ending in the life cycle of a quilt, mind you. You can add patches and loving stitches as it is worn by time. Your children and grandchildren can repair it. The curious person who finds it at a thrift store can repair it.

To pause our soft work of reckoning with life online, let's stitch together the care and curiosity you've offered yourself here. Cut out each of your quilt squares and arrange them in the space on the next page. "Bind" your quilt by drawing a border that holds your squares together. What color, texture, or pattern feels right to contain this process?

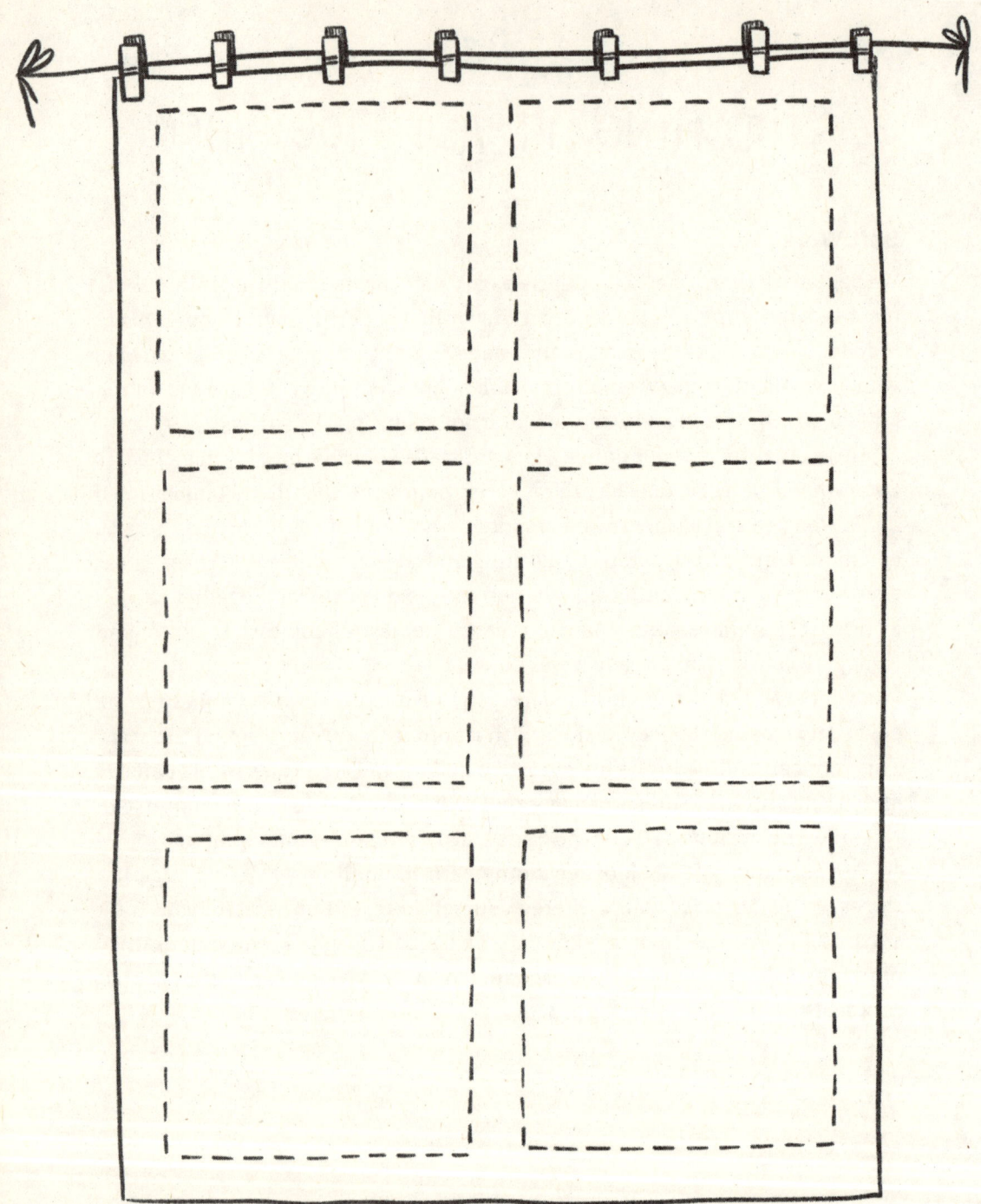

Reflect:

Imagine you are holding this quilt in your hands.

› What does it feel like against your skin?

_____
_____

› How do you feel when it's wrapped around your body?

_____
_____

› Who would you invite to sit under it with you?

_____
_____

› What prize would it win at a county fair?

_____
_____

Draw your prize ribbon here:

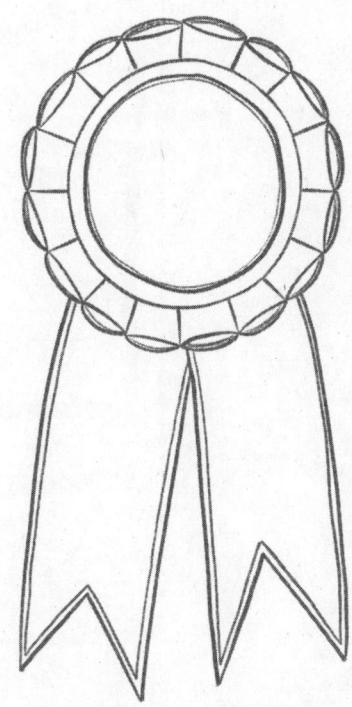

STITCHING IT ALL TOGETHER

Playlist: Songs for Thriving Online

Compile the songs you chose at the end of each chapter into one playlist. Listen to your playlist as you move through your day. What do you notice about this collection of music? Do certain themes or genres recur? Does the playlist travel between many different moods and personalities? You can change the order or add songs to tell a new story.

Imagine the cover art for this playlist as a whole.

Celebrate Yourself

Throw a party in honor of the effort you've brought to this workbook! Cut out the gifts you drew yourself at the end of each chapter and arrange them below. Decorate the party in any way that feels celebratory to you.

Reflect:

Imagine this is a surprise party and that you are the guest of honor. When you walk through the door and see the selection of gifts, what would you guess the theme of this gathering is?

› The theme of this party is:

_____

Inhabit the Future

Write the story of a day in your life ten years from now. Give yourself permission to dream big. This future doesn't need to be practical or realistic. As you author a vision for a future you would like to inhabit, consider:

› How does technology fit into the rhythm of my day?
› What does social media make easy?
› What do I enjoy most online?
› How do platforms work differently than they do today?
› When do I pick up my phone? What am I doing when I'm not online?

_____
_____
_____
_____
_____
_____
_____

Go back and read the story you've just written and circle all your favorite words. Choose five that feel the most important to you

1. _____

2. _____

3. _____

4. _____

5. _____

Reflect:

How do these words already exist in your life today? Write a sentence with each word that feels true today.

Word 1: _____
_____
_____

Word 2: _____
_____
_____

Word 3: _____
_____
_____

Word 4: _____
_____
_____

Word 5: _____
_____
_____

The Gentle Manifesto

A manifesto is testimony of what we believe and how we wish to engage with life. Artistic manifestos might describe the philosophy or rules behind a creative practice. Political manifestos might speak truth to power or call for revolution. What makes this manifesto different is that it won't make demands or criticize you for following it imperfectly. Instead of a binding contract, imagine it as a lantern illuminating the trailhead of a future worth creating. You might choose language that refers directly to your relationship with social media. You might also write broadly, illustrating the vastness of what well-being means to you. Allow your Gentle Manifesto to serve as a beacon of your personal values and your unique rendering of what it means to feel well, online and offline.

Each of the following sentences corresponds to one chapter in this workbook. Flip back through the pages of each chapter, have a visit with your art and reflections, and complete each phrase.

> CHAPTER 1 | ATTENTION
> Today I feel most like myself when I'm paying attention to:

_____

_____

_____

> CHAPTER 2 | PRODUCTIVITY + URGENCY
> Today I redefine *success* to mean:

_____

_____

_____

› CHAPTER 3 | PRIVACY + PERFORMANCE
Today the type of vulnerability that feels empowering is:

_____
_____
_____

› CHAPTER 4 | COMPARISON + WORTHINESS
Today I can recognize my inherent worthiness when:

_____
_____
_____

› CHAPTER 5 | FEAR + ANGER + DISINFORMATION
Today my fear and anger can be safely held by:

_____
_____
_____

› CHAPTER 6 | PLACE + BODY + BELONGING
Today I experience true connection when:

_____
_____
_____

Action Menu

Online, what actions support each of these statements? Brainstorm the choices, habits, and hacks that could help you live the values of your Gentle Manifesto. These might be rituals you already practice, things you could imagine trying, or bold steps that could be taken in the future. You don't *need* to do any of these things. A menu is simply a gallery of possibilities.

Today, I feel most like myself when I'm paying attention to:

_____

On social media, this can look like:

1. _____
2. _____
3. _____
4. _____
5. _____

Today I redefine *success* to mean:

_____

On social media, this can look like:

1. _____
2. _____
3. _____
4. _____
5. _____

Today, the type of vulnerability that feels empowering is:

_____

On social media, this can look like:

1. _____
2. _____
3. _____
4. _____
5. _____

Today, I can recognize my inherent worthiness when:

_____

On social media, this can look like:

1. _____
2. _____
3. _____
4. _____
5. _____

Today, my fear and anger can be safely held by:

_____

On social media, this can look like:

1. _____
2. _____
3. _____
4. _____
5. _____

Today, I experience true connection when:

_____

On social media, this can look like:

1. _____
2. _____
3. _____
4. _____
5. _____

Compassion in Action

If you're planning to explore shifting how you relate to social media, then accompany your goals for change with a plan for self-compassion. Don't let the richness of your journey be interrupted by the false idols of discipline and perfectionistic follow-through. What you take away from this workbook has nothing to do with:

› how flawlessly you implement a life-changing new habit
› the fervor of your resolve to change
› certainty about what hacks or habits will work forever
› your ability to sustain motivation

Let's say you decide a month away from social media would feel nourishing. Then two weeks from now you come down with the flu and find yourself indulging in videos of dogs reacting to babies arriving home from the hospital. (In my book, that's always time well spent.) Or maybe you intend on keeping your phone in the kitchen drawer at night from now on, but on day two, you realize you've brought it to bed out of habit. Perhaps you've already had the experience of trying to regulate your screen time during the uncertainty and isolation of a global health crisis.

Reflect:

› How have I spoken to myself in the past when I've "failed"?

_____

› What can I imagine saying to myself instead?

_____

› What reminds me of my values and intentions?

_____

› What "shoulds" are not welcome in my evolving definition of well-being?

_____

› What simple, creative act brings me back to center?

_____

Here is another paradox of healing: you can dream boldly of a future that looks different from today *and* be unwavering in the kindness you offer to yourself in moments of shame, frustration, and disappointment.

You are allowed to change your mind about what works for you. You are allowed to try something different. You are allowed to pivot without owing anyone an explanation or apology. You are allowed to forgive yourself when social media impacts you exactly the way it was designed to. The standard you hold yourself to today may not fit the shape of your life tomorrow. Instead of asking, "Why can't I just put down my phone?!," a more compassionate inquiry might be, "How do I want to be *with* myself when the path is not linear?"

Where shame builds a barricade, compassion is a gentle usher who smiles, flicks on their flashlight, and leads us back to our seats in the auditorium of worthiness and belonging.

CONCLUSION

THIS IS A PAUSE, not an ending.

If this workbook didn't fix you, then you are in good company. If you have unresolved questions, frustrations, and ideas, then that is proof you have been present with yourself. You have spent more than 260 pages getting curious enough about your evolving relationship with social media to build the foundation of an inquiry that will span a lifetime. Becoming attuned to oneself is so much more useful than searching for a singular hack that "fixes" you.

Parts of this workbook will be outdated by the time you read these words—my pen doesn't write at the speed of technological innovation fueled by capitalism. Being among the first generations to grapple with life online, I suspect our early musings will seem simple as the path of humanity is rapidly transformed by technology.

Perhaps one day each of us will be fortunate enough to become elders who know children who giggle at descriptions of the devices we carried or the concept of a hashtag. Maybe we will find it funny too. And perhaps we will say, with self-forgiveness and generosity, that it was confusing to exist in an era when these tools were new and the culture around them was still deciding what it would be. We might say that it was hard or terrifying. We might also say that it was thrilling, and that sometimes it revealed the best of ourselves. Then maybe our words will slow, in that deliberate way wise people speak when something is really true: *What mattered in the confusion and terror and thrill of it all wasn't really about navigating social media; it was about making peace with our imperfect selves.*

Thriving online is not a question of what you do or don't do with your phone. It is, instead, a daily return to the living animal of your body and listening to it with an attention that defies urgency. It is saying kind words to that fallible self when it has been susceptible to excess or promises of relief from the task of human-being. Thriving is not always the product of solutions. It is sometimes changing your mind. Or forgiving yourself for however long it took to see clearly. And then forgiving yourself again for arriving at clarity the hard way. The art of thriving online is the practice of inhabiting place and returning over and over when we are pulled away. It is sharing that land with other people and their complicated wholeness. You don't have to do this all at once. In fact, we can't. What a relief.

So, instead of an ending, this final page is only an invitation to pause,
to celebrate the moments of contemplation you have gifted to yourself—
your soft work of being curious—
and the open invitation to continue returning to the question
of what well-being can mean for you.

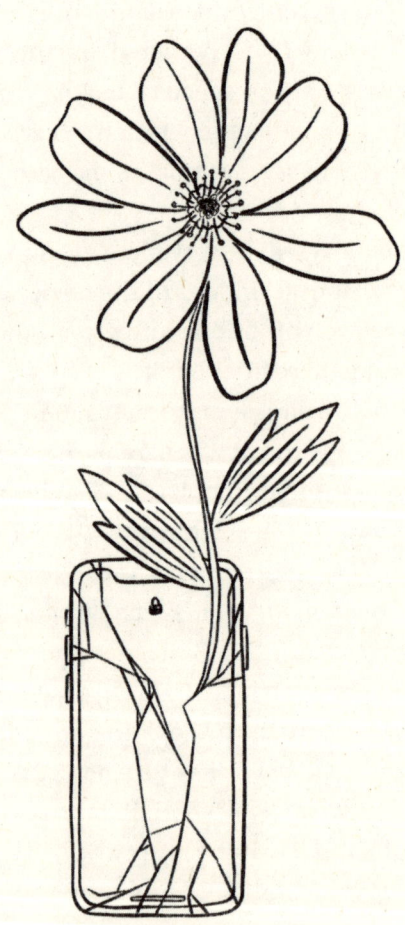

Acknowledgments

I'D LIKE TO THANK the internet for being weird and frustrating and fascinating enough to hold my attention. Thank you to anyone who paused their scrolling and joined into conversations with me on social media. This book is for us.

To my mentors and peers at the Kutenai Art Therapy Institute, especially Millie Cumming, for teaching me how to forge my own moral compass.

To my agent, Laura Mazer, the warm advocate and birth partner of this project. To my editors, Diana Ventimiglia, Angela Wix, Jade Lascelles, and Laurel Kallenbach, for being this book's enthusiastic test subjects. To Jennifer Miles, Charli Barnes, and the art team for bringing the illustrations on these pages to life. I am so incredibly grateful to everyone at Sounds True. Thank you for your trust and stewardship.

To my circle of friends in Slocan who let me read passages of this book at parties. And also to my internet friends turned real.

To my mother, who pioneered vulnerability in public, and to the rest of my family, who cared for me on the long journey of this project.

To my husband, who *really listened* to fragmented chapters at the end of his own long days and was the safe harbor to rebuild myself within.

To my dog, Pants, who takes me for walks outside when I've been staring at a screen for too long.

Notes

Acknowledging the Land

1. *Truth and Reconciliation Commission of Canada: Calls to Action*, Truth and Reconciliation Commission of Canada (2015), downloadable PDF www2.gov.bc.ca/assets/gov/british-columbians-our-governments/indigenous-people/aboriginal-peoples-documents/calls_to_action_english2.pdf.
2. *United Nations Declaration on the Rights of Indigenous Peoples*, adopted by the General Assembly, September 2007, UN.org/development/desa/indigenouspeoples/wp-content/uploads/sites/19/2018/11/UNDRIP_E_web.pdf.

Content Warning

1. "Find a Helpline," International Association for Suicide Prevention, accessed May 9, 2024, iasp.info/crisis-centres-helplines. Find a Helpline is a free online tool that easily connects people to helplines in more than fifty countries.

Introduction

1. Nicholas Jackson, "United Nations Declares Internet Access a Basic Human Right," *The Atlantic*, June 3, 2011, theatlantic.com/technology/archive/2011/06/united-nations-declares-internet-access-a-basic-human-right/239911.
2. *Report of the Special Rapporteur on the Promotion and Protection of the Right to Freedom of Opinion and Expression*, United Nations Commission on Human Rights, 2011, www2.ohchr.org/english/bodies/hrcouncil/docs/17session/A.HRC.17.27_en.pdf.

Chapter 1: Attention

1. Jenny Odell, *How to Do Nothing: Resisting the Attention Economy* (New York: Melville House Publishing, 2019), xi.
2. Mike Allen, "Sean Parker Unloads on Facebook: 'God Only Knows What It's Doing to Our Children's Brains,'" Axios, November 9, 2017, axios.com/2017/12/15/sean-parker-unloads-on-facebook-god-only-knows-what-its-doing-to-our-childrens-brains-1513306792.

Chapter 2: Productivity + Urgency

1. Nicholas Bloom, "How Working from Home Works Out," Stanford Institute for Economic Policy Research, June 2020, siepr.stanford.edu/publications/policy-brief/how-working-home-works-out.
2. Derek Thompson, "The Great Resignation Is Accelerating," *The Atlantic*, October 15, 2021, theatlantic.com/ideas/archive/2021/10/great-resignation-accelerating/620382/.
3. Philip Hamilton, "Stop Glamorizing 'the Grind' and Start Glamorizing Whatever This Is," *Know Your Meme*, August 5, 2022, knowyourmeme.com/memes/stop-glamorizing-the-grind-and-start-glamorizing-whatever-this-is.
4. Tricia Hersey, *Rest Is Resistance* (New York: Little, Brown Spark, 2022), 7.
5. "Lazy," *Online Etymology Dictionary*, accessed November 27, 2023, etymonline/search?q=lazy.
6. Devon Price, *Laziness Does Not Exist* (New York: Atria Books, 2021), 22.
7. "Housing 'Out of Reach' for Bay Area Minimum-Wage Workers: Report," NBC's *Bay City News*, July 29, 2022, nbcbayarea.com/news/local/bay-area-housing-minimum-wage-workers/2963777/.
8. Herbert J. Freudenberger, "The Staff Burn-Out Syndrome in Alternative Institutions," *Psychotherapy: Theory, Research & Practice*, 12, no. 1 (1975): 73–82, doi.org/10.1037/h0086411.
9. Saundra Dalton-Smith, "The Real Reason Why We Are Tired and What to Do About It," TEDxAtlanta, March 2019, youtube.com/watch?v=ZGNN4EPJzGk&t=63s.
10. Saundra Dalton-Smith, *Sacred Rest* (London: Hachette UK, 2017).
11. Tiffany Shlain, *24/6: The Power of Unplugging One Day a Week* (New York: Gallery Books/Simon & Schuster, 2019), 7.

Chapter 3: Privacy + Performance

1. Rhitu Chatterjee, "Where Did Agriculture Begin? Oh Boy, It's Complicated," NPR, July 15, 2016, npr.org/sections/thesalt/2016/07/15/485722228/where-did-agriculture-begin-oh-boy-its-complicated.
2. Maya Wei-Haas, "This 45,500-Year-Old Pig Painting Is the World's Oldest Animal Art," *National Geographic*, January 13, 2021, nationalgeographic.com/science/article/45500-year-old-pig-painting-worlds-oldest-animal-art#:~:text=Some%2045%2C500%20years%20ago%2C%20on.
3. Irvin D. Yalom and Molyn Leszcz, *The Theory and Practice of Group Psychotherapy*, 5th ed. (New York: Basic Books, 2005), 6.

4. Carter Dougherty, "Polaroid Lovers Try to Revive Its Instant Film," *New York Times*, May 25, 2009, Technology section, nytimes.com/2009/05/26/technology/26polaroid.html.
5. Cody Cook-Parrott, "Intimacy Portals," *Monday Monday*, Substack, February 13, 2023, codycookparrott.substack.com/p/intimacy-portals?utm_source=profile&utm_medium=reader2.
6. Shoshana Zuboff, *The Age of Surveillance Capitalism: The Fight for a Human Future at the New Frontier of Power* (New York: Public Affairs, 2019).
7. Nadeem Badshah, "Facebook to Contact 87 Million Users Affected by Data Breach," *The Guardian*, April 9, 2018, theguardian.com/technology/2018/apr/08/facebook-to-contact-the-87-million-users-affected-by-data-breach.
8. Christopher Wylie, *Mindf*ck: Cambridge Analytica and the Plot to Break America* (New York: Random House, 2019), 96.
9. 7amleh, "The Attacks on Palestinian Digital Rights," The Arab Center for the Advancement of Social Media, 2021, 7amleh.org/storage/The%20Attacks%20on%20Palestinian%20Digital%20Rights.pdf.
10. 7amlaeh, "The Attacks on Palestinian Digital Rights."
11. Lenard Monkman, "Indigenous Women's Instagram Stories on MMIWG Awareness Vanish on Red Dress Day," CBC, May 7, 2021, cbc.ca/news/indigenous/instagram-stories-vanish-mmiwg-red-dress-day-1.6017113.
12. OpenAI, ChatGPT (large language model), accessed May 11, 2023, chatgpt.com.

Chapter 4: Comparison + Worthiness

1. Leon Festinger, "A Theory of Social Comparison Processes," *Human Relations* 7, no. 2 (1954): 117–40, doi.org/10.1177/001872675400700202.
2. Ethan Zell and Mark D. Alicke, "The Local Dominance Effect in Self-Evaluation: Evidence and Explanations," *Personality and Social Psychology Review* 14, no. 4 (2010): 368–84, doi.org/10.1177/1088868310366144.
3. J. P. Gerber, Ladd Wheeler, and Jerry Suls, "A Social Comparison Theory Meta-Analysis 60+ Years On," *Psychological Bulletin* 144, no. 2 (2018): 177–9, doi.org/10.1037/bul0000127.
4. Hillary Kaplan, "It's Giving Uncanny Valley," TikTok, February 28, 2023, tiktok.com/@subversivesocialite/video/7205332409548541190?is_from_webapp=1&web_id=7114825074759222790.
5. Masahiro Mori, Karl MacDorman, and Norri Kageki, "The Uncanny Valley [from the Field]," *IEEE Robotics & Automation Magazine* 19, no. 2 (June 2012): 98–100, doi.org/10.1109/mra.2012.2192811.

6. Mori, MacDorman, and Kageki, "The Uncanny Valley [from the Field]."
7. Rhona Christie, "Thoughts on How Filters Affect How We Feel," March 5, 2023, tiktok.com/@rhonachristie/video/7207074770821696774.
8. Risa Gelles-Watnick, "Americans' Use of Mobile Technology and Home Broadband," Pew Research Center: Internet, Science & Tech, January 31, 2024, pewresearch.org/internet/2024/01/31/americans-use-of-mobile-technology-and-home-broadband/.

Chapter 5: Fear + Anger + Disinformation

1. Richard C. Schwartz, *No Bad Parts: Healing Trauma and Restoring Wholeness with the Internal Family Systems Model* (Boulder, CO: Sounds True, 2021): 12.
2. Noam Lapidot-Lefler and Azy Barak, "Effects of Anonymity, Invisibility, and Lack of Eye-Contact on Toxic Online Disinhibition," *Computers in Human Behavior* 28, no. 2 (2012): 434–43, doi.org/10.1016/j.chb.2011.10.014.
3. Nina Jankowicz, *How to Be a Woman Online: Surviving Abuse and Harassment, and How to Fight Back* (London: Bloomsbury Academic), 4–42.
4. Paul Mozur, "A Genocide Incited on Facebook, with Posts from Myanmar's Military," *New York Times*, October 15, 2018, nytimes.com/2018/10/15/technology/myanmar-facebook-genocide.html.
5. Max Fisher, *The Chaos Machine: The Inside Story of How Social Media Rewired Our Minds and Our World* (New York: Little, Brown and Company, 2022), 13–137.
6. Emmet Lyons, "Elon Musk's X Platform Fueled Far-Right Riots in Ireland, Experts Say," CBS News, December 5, 2023, cbsnews.com/news/elon-musk-ireland-x-twitter-far-right-dublin-immigration.
7. William J. Brady, Julian A. Wills, John T. Jost, Joshua A. Tucker, and Jay J. Van Bavel, "Emotion Shapes the Diffusion of Moralized Content in Social Networks," *Proceedings of the National Academy of Sciences* 114, no. 28 (2017), doi.org/10.1073/pnas.1618923114.
8. Jari Kätsyri, Teemu Kinnunen, Kenta Kusumoto, Pirkko Oittinen, and Niklas Ravaja, "Negativity Bias in Media Multitasking: The Effects of Negative Social Media Messages on Attention to Television News Broadcasts," edited by Eldad Yechiam, *PLOS ONE* 11, no. 5 (2016): 2–3, doi.org/10.1371/journal.pone.0153712.
9. Henri Tajifel and John C. Turner, "Social Psychology of Intergroup Relations," *Annual Review of Psychology* 33 (February 1982), doi.org/10.1146/annurev.ps.33.020182.000245.

10. Christopher Wylie, *Mindf*ck: Cambridge Analytica and the Plot to Break America* (New York: Random House, 2019), 77.
11. Elizabeth Kolbert, "Why Facts Don't Change Our Minds," *New Yorker*, February 19, 2017, newyorker.com/magazine/2017/02/27/why-facts-dont-change-our-minds.
12. Wylie, *Mindf*ck*, 67.
13. Emma Graham-Harrison and Carole Cadwalladr, "Revealed: 50 Million Facebook Profiles Harvested for Cambridge Analytica in Major Data Breach," *The Guardian*, March 17, 2018, theguardian.com/news/2018/mar/17/cambridge-analytica-facebook-influence-us-election.
14. *The Great Hack*, directed by Jehane Noujaim and Karim Amer (Netflix, 2019).

Chapter 6: Place + Body + Belonging

1. Anna Ciaunica, Luke McEllin, Julian Kiverstein, Vittorio Gallese, Jakob Hohwy, and Mateusz Woźniak, "Zoomed Out: Digital Media Use and Depersonalization Experiences during the COVID-19 Lockdown," *Scientific Reports* 12, no. 1 (2022), doi.org/10.1038/s41598-022-07657-8.
2. Kelly Diels, "The Dangers of Fake Community," *Sunday Love Letter* (blog), February 12, 2013, kellydiels.com/.
3. Anna Seirian, email message to author, September 3, 2023.
4. Anna Lembke, *Dopamine Nation: Resetting Your Brain in the Age of Cheap Pleasures* (New York: Dutton, 2021), 53.
5. Resmaa Menakem, *My Grandmother's Hands: Racialized Trauma and the Pathway to Mending Our Hearts and Bodies* (Las Vegas: Central Recovery Press, 2017), 12.
6. David Whyte, *Everything Is Waiting for You: Poems* (Langley, WA: Many Rivers Press, 2003).
7. Joanna Macy and Molly Young Brown, *Coming Back to Life: Practices to Reconnect Our Lives, Our World* (Gabriola Island, BC: New Society Publishers, 1998), 39–40.
8. Margery Williams, "The Velveteen Rabbit," *Harper's Bazaar* 56, no. 6 (June 1921), archive.org/details/sim_harpers-bazaar_1921-06_56_6/page/72/mode/2up.

Book Club Guide

HERE ARE A FEW IDEAS for how you could complete this workbook in community:

› Plan a weekly meetup with friends, family, or coworkers. Everyone will go through a chapter alone each week. When you gather, go around the circle and share your harvest exercises.
› Make your book club an event! Cook together or pack a picnic. Cover a table with paper so you can all doodle while you share.
› Start a group chat to share screenshots and links that remind you of the week's theme.
› Have one person host each meeting by choosing a piece of online content that relates to the chapter. Use a post, meme, video, or article to spark discussion.
› End meetups with time to make art together while listening to the music from everyone's playlists. Each week, color or decorate a petal from the template on the following page.
› At your final meetup, draw a circle on a large piece of paper. Have everyone write their Gentle Manifesto inside.
› Have everyone cut out all their petals and assemble them around the circle into a blooming, collective expression of your shared journey.
› Together, fill the background of the paper with drawings, collage images, and phrases to encourage one another.
› Take a picture of your collaborative art, and make it the profile picture of a group chat. Use that space to share thoughts, art, and content to keep the discussion alive.

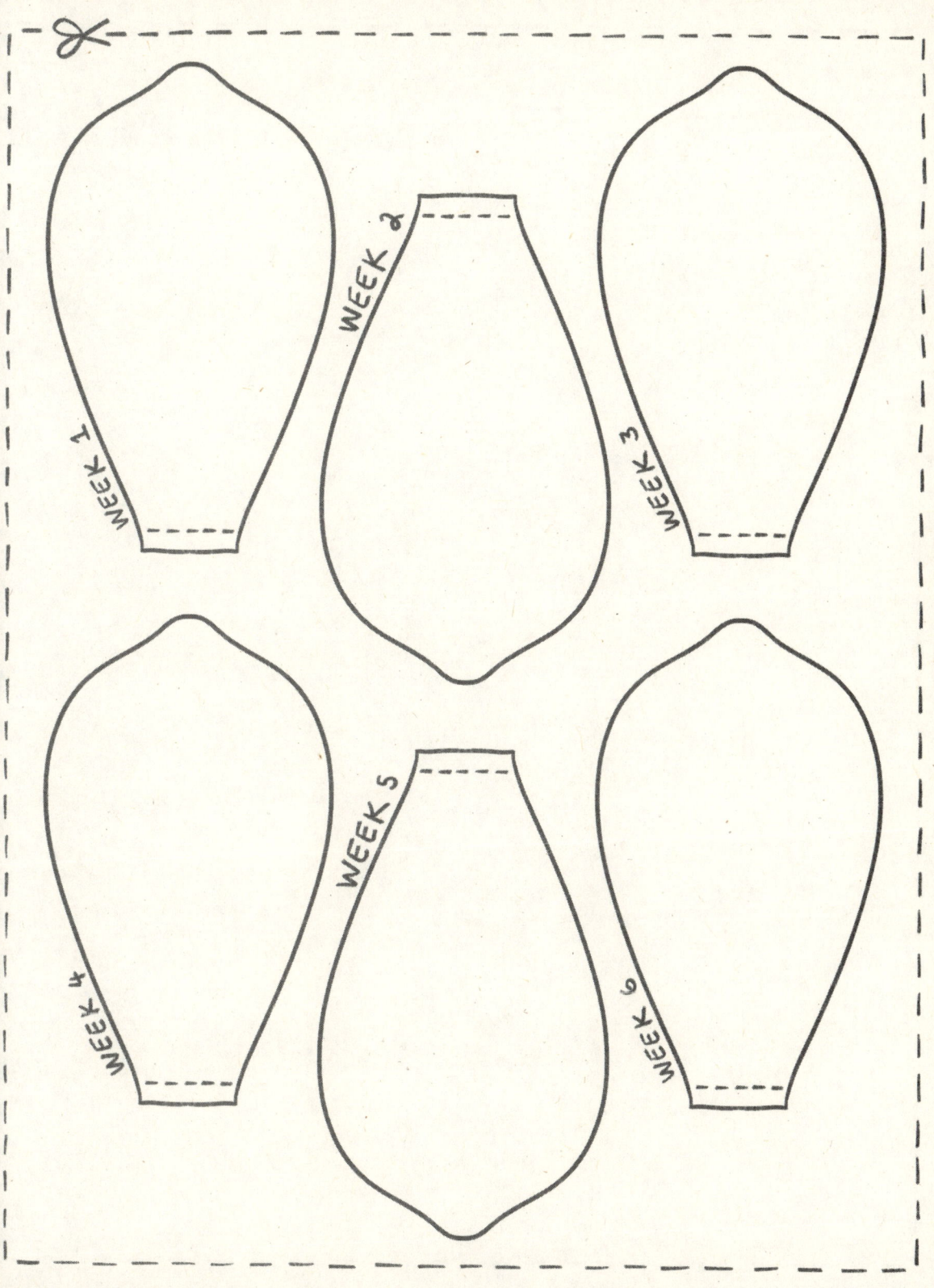

SNIP! SNIP!

About the Author

AMELIA KNOTT is a Registered Psychotherapist and art therapist who specializes in the mental health impacts of hustle culture and the attention economy. She studied interdisciplinary art at the Maryland Institute College of Art in Baltimore before returning home to Canada to train at the Kutenai Art Therapy Institute in Nelson, British Columbia. She describes herself as being chronically online, using social media to challenge the status quo of the wellness industry, and advocating for digital ethics and creativity as a force for healing. The walls of Amelia's home studio in Slocan, British Columbia, are covered in half-finished paintings and poems. She learned to quilt while writing this book.

Learn more about Amelia's online therapeutic art groups and workshops: arttherapyinreallife.com.

Amelia would love to see what you create inside this workbook! If it feels good to share, tag her on TikTok and Instagram: @Art_Therapy_IRL and find inspiration for your next art project.

About Sounds True

SOUNDS TRUE was founded in 1985 by Tami Simon with a clear mission: to disseminate spiritual wisdom. Since starting out as a project with one woman and her tape recorder, we have grown into a multimedia publishing company with a catalog of more than 3,000 titles by some of the leading teachers and visionaries of our time, and an ever-expanding family of beloved customers from across the world.

In more than three decades of evolution, Sounds True has maintained our focus on our overriding purpose and mission: to wake up the world. We offer books, audio programs, online learning experiences, and in-person events to support your personal growth and awakening, and to unlock our greatest human capacities to love and serve.

At SoundsTrue.com you'll find a wealth of resources to enrich your journey, including our weekly *Insights at the Edge* podcast, free downloads, and information about our nonprofit Sounds True Foundation, where we strive to remove financial barriers to the materials we publish through scholarships and donations worldwide.

To learn more, please visit SoundsTrue.com/freegifts or call us toll-free at 800.333.9185.

Together, we can wake up the world.